RUGBY
A Pictorial History

A view of High Street in about 1900, from a painting by Cynthia Chandler.

RUGBY
A Pictorial History

E. W. Timmins

Phillimore

1990

Published by
PHILLIMORE & CO. LTD.
Shopwyke Hall, Chichester, Sussex

ISBN 0 85033 700 3

Printed and bound in Great Britain by
BIDDLES LTD.
Guildford, Surrey

List of Illustrations

Frontispiece: Painting of High Street, *c*.1900

Introduction
1. Map showing surviving Iron Age settlements
2. Three faces of the shaft of an eighth-century cross
3. Plan of 15th-century Rugby
4. The medieval open-field system

Market Place
5. The *George Inn* and church, *c*.1810
6. The *George Hotel*, 1876
7. Market day, *c*.1905
8. Market Place, *c*.1900
9. View from the *George Hotel*, 1895
10. Ladies crossing Market Place, 1895
11. Street-piano, Market Place, 1896
12. The yellow fly outside the *George Hotel*, 1896
13. Market Place in the 1880s
14. Corner of Chapel Street and Market Place in 1894
15. The Co-op premises in Chapel Street, 1910

North Street
16. The Beatty Survey of the North Street area
17. The top of North Street, 1896
18. Thatched cottages in North Street, *c*.1910
19. Back view of cottage No.11 in 1924
20. Boughton House in 1888
21. Boughton House decorated for Jubilee celebrations, 1887
22. The drawing-room, Boughton House, 1888
23. Bennfield House
24. Rear view of Bennfield House
25. North Street decorated for the Diamond Jubilee, 1897
26. Regency house in North Street
27. Beatty Survey of the west side of North Street, 1851
28. Lower west side of North Street, 1897
29. Cottage garden behind North Street
30. Cottage in North Street, 1902
31. Rugby Lodge, *c*.1895
32. Caldecott Park, *c*.1910
33. J. J. Webster, a local carrier
34. The *Avon Mill Inn*, 1897

Church Street
35. The old Lawrence Sheriff Almshouses
36. Church Street, *c*.1900
37. Castle Street from Church Street, 1901
38. No.17 Church Street, drawn in 1867 by J. H. Hollier
39. No.55 Church Street, *c*.1900
40. Holy Trinity Church
41. North side of Church Street, *c*.1865
42. Church Street in 1878

Gas Street
43. View from the top of the Trinity Church tower, 1880
44. The Baptist Chapel before 1805
45. Hospital in Castle Street
46. No.18 Gas Street
47. Cottages in Pinder's Lane, 1896

Sheep Street
48. Sheep Street, *c*.1873
49. South end of Sheep Street, *c*.1910
50. Sheep Street in 1895
51. Sheep Street from Dukes' yard, *c*.1880
52. Sheep Street, *c*.1902
53. Etching of the Shambles in 1802
54. Lower Sheep Street in the Beatty Survey of 1850/1
55. J. G. Sylvester's stall at No.2 the Shambles, *c*.1888
56. Sheasby's drapery and haberdashery, *c*.1905
57. Mrs. Taverner's millinery in Sheep Street in 1890

High Street
58. High Street in 1826 by Edward Pretty
59. Aquatint of the High Street made in 1843
60. High Street and Sheep Street in the Beatty Survey
61. Engraving of the Town Hall, 1864
62. Rugby School, 1890
63. High Street in 1912
64. The *Shoulder of Mutton*, 1896
65. The Benn Building
66. High Street, *c*.1912

Lawrence Sheriff Street
67. Corner of Sheep Street and School Street in 1851
68. Cottages at the corner of School Street in the 1860s
69. Engraving of School Street in 1865
70. Drawing of High Street in 1885
71. Elborowe's House in 1890
72. Elborowe's House soon after 1896
73. Corner of Drury Lane and Lawrence Sheriff Street, c.1923

Warwick Street and Bilton Road
74. Aerial view from Rugby School Chapel tower, c.1880
75. Warwick Street and Addison Row, c.1912
76. Warwick Street and Rugby School, c.1912
77. Drawing of Butlin's Mound, 1888
78. Oakfield House in 1914
79. Cyclist passing the *Star Inn*, 1896
80. Bilton Road corner in 1902
81. Repairs to Bilton Road in 1906
82. Watercolour of the view at the foot of Bilton Hill, 1838

Clifton Road
83. Cattle in Clifton Road, c.1903
84. Midland Red buses in Clifton Road in 1926
85. Clifton Road beyond Paradise Street, c.1908
86. Family walking along Clifton Road in 1896
87. Lower School, Clifton Road, 1903
88. Whitehall, Whitehall Road, 1865
89. Clifton Road leading out of town, c.1900
90. Drawing of Butler's Leap, c.1885

Hillmorton Road
91. Aerial view of Hillmorton Road, c.1880
92. Hillmorton Road and the Recreation Ground in 1910
93. First World War tank in the Recreation Ground
94. Lane leading to Lower Hillmorton in 1910

Streets to the Station
95. Railway Terrace in 1880
96. The Palace Theatre, 1911
97. Albert Street in 1908
98. Regent Street, c.1912
99. Cattle market at the bottom of Railway Terrace, 1903

Dunchurch and Barby Roads
100. The Catholic Church in Dunchurch Road in 1864
101. Dunchurch Road in 1890

102. St Marie's Church, c.1910
103. The Laurels in 1900
104. Barby Road, c.1906
105. Water tower in Barby Road
106. The water tower in 1902

The Rural Scene
107. Drawing of Onley Fields in 1884
108. Drawing of the Avon near Newbold in 1882
109. Abbot's Farm, 1938
110. The Oxford Canal near Brownsover

St Andrew's Church
111. Plan of St Andrew's Church made in 1766
112. Drawing of the church by G. Mayes
113. Early 14th-century chest in St Andrew's
114. South side of St Andrew's Church in 1826
115. North side of the church in 1864
116. The church interior in 1870
117. Interior of the church looking west
118. Construction of the new tower and spire in 1894
119. The old Rectory House
120. The rectory plan in the Beatty Survey of 1851

Rugby School
121. South front of Rugby School in 1809
122. The south front in 1825
123. Drawing of Rugby School from School Street
124. Aquatint of Rugby School in 1817
125. The school from Barby Road, c.1880
126. Statue of Thomas Hughes, c.1910

The Railways
127. Constructing the embankment at Hillmorton in 1837
128. View over the embankment to Rugby by Edward Rudge
129. Etching of the viaduct, c.1860
130. The station in Railway Terrace, c.1860
131. Train at the L.N.W.R. station in 1910
132. The signal gantry, 1896
133. Construction of the Great Central Railway bridge in 1896
134. The Great Central station, Hillmorton Road, 1910

Institutions
135. Staff leaving the B.T.H. Company offices, c.1912
136. The Rugby Portland Cement Works, 1890
137. The Hospital of St Cross, 1903
138. View of the hospital from the south in 1905
139. The hospital: Sun Pavilion
140. The men's ward in 1905
141. The Rugby Fire Brigade in 1876
142. The Rugby Football Club fifteen in 1878

143. The Rugby Cricket Club side in 1894
144. The Rugby Town Football Club in the 1911-12 season

Events
145. The last use of the stocks, 1865
146. Claude Grahame-White landing his biplane, 1910
147. High Street decorated for Edward VII's visit in 1909
148. Regent Street decorated for the same occasion
149. Memorial service for Edward VII, 1910

150. Armistice parade at the Recreation Ground, 1918
151. Armistice march-past, 1918
152. Service at the Clock Tower to celebrate the Armistice
153. Unveiling the War Memorial Gates, 1922
154. Thanksgiving service in the Market Place, 1897
155. Queen Victoria's Diamond Jubilee, 1897
156. Visit of Edward VII, 1909
157. Celebrating George V's Silver Jubilee, 1935
158. The Clock Tower decorated for Elizabeth II's coronation, 1953

Acknowledgements

Over my long years of research I have come to owe a great debt of gratitude to so many people for their help that it is not practicable to record their names individually, but I include them in my sincere thanks to the authorities and staff of the following: in London, the Public Record Office and the British Library and Manuscript Room; the Record Offices at Bedford, Coventry, Leicester, Lichfield, Lincoln, Northampton, Stafford, Stratford-on-Avon Shakespeare Centre and Warwick; the libraries or museums at Birmingham, Coventry, Leicester, Market Harborough, Northampton, the Northamptonshire Record Society, Rugby School, Warwick, the Rugby Borough Council Legal Department, Rugby Local History Research Group, and, in particular, the Rugby Public Library. Finally I have to thank my wife Margaret for her great patience and her invaluable assistance in my researches.

Grateful acknowledgement is made to the following for permission to reproduce copyright material for the illustrations: Rugby Public Library, 5, 6, 10, 11, 13, 16, 17, 19, 20-28, 30, 31, 33, 34, 36-39, 41-43, 45, 46, 48, 51, 55, 59, 60, 62, 64, 65, 72-74, 83, 84, 87, 88, 91, 93, 100-3, 106, 110, 115-18, 120, 125, 126, 130, 132, 134, 136, 141-3, 152, 153, 155, 157, 158; Warwickshire Record Office, 7, 8, 12, 14, 15, 18, 32, 35, 49, 50, 52, 56, 66, 75, 76, 78, 81, 85, 89, 92, 94-99, 104, 111, 131, 135, 137-40, 144, 146-51, 156; Rugby School, 58, 67, 69, 70, 90, 107, 108, 121, 123; Bedfordshire Record Office, 122; Bedford Museums, 82, 127, 128; Society of Antiquaries of London, 2; Miss P. Goodman, 57; Mrs. A. Aliberti, 65; Mr. N. Smith, 29; Maidstone Museum and Art Gallery for the drawing at the end of the Introduction. The remainder are supplied by the author.

Preface

Previous books on the history of Rugby have tended to devote more attention to Rugby School than to the town itself, partly as a result of its greater fame, but also because it was better documented. This book is based on more than a quarter of a century of extensive and on-going research into original sources, and is an attempt to redress the balance by presenting a synopsis of the long history of the town of Rugby in an accessible form, with an abundance of illustrations which are now in themselves historical records. I have taken great care to ensure the reliability of the information included, but if there should be any inaccuracies, I tender my apologies, although further research is bound to reveal the need for some modifications. Due to the pictorial nature of this volume, a full apparatus of reference is not possible, but I hope in the future to produce a more textual account. In the meantime I trust that this volume will open the eyes of many to what still lies about them in Rugby, and will succeed in engendering a greater awareness of our historical heritage and a desire for its preservation.

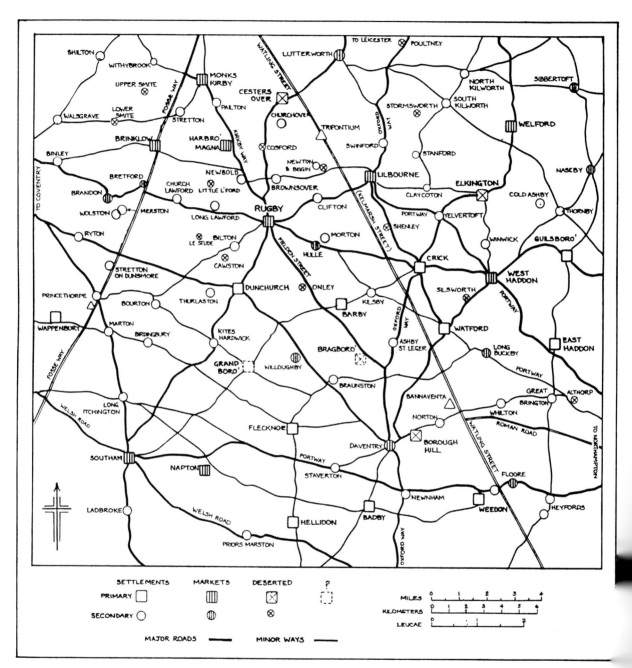

1. The map shows the pattern of surviving early (Iron Age) settlements set in the ancient network of roads, many of which are still in use. The position of Rugby at a focal point is clear, as is its encirclement by later Saxon villages. Some stretches of road are now only footpaths, or have vanished altogether, but the line of Watling Street cutting across the old road system stands out as if it were a modern motorway.

Introduction

'No man is an Iland, intire of it selfe' (John Donne)

The words of the poet in their broader sense have a special significance in the study of history, and in the case of Rugby, its early history in particular has become clearer only through ceasing to treat it as an 'Iland'. Archaeology has produced little evidence for the activities of early man in Rugby or its vicinity, due mainly to destruction by ploughing from Saxon times, extensive building during the last 200 years, and more recently, through drastic changes in farming practice in the countryside. However, a lack of evidence does not prove the history of that period to be a blank.

No systematic archaeological excavation has been made on any site in the town itself, and such finds as have occurred were made generally before the turn of the century and often by chance. They ranged from Bronze Age to Medieval, but cannot themselves lead to any firm conclusions about the origins of the town. Since the 1820s it has been supposed that Rugby was originally a small Iron-Age hill-fort occupied by members of the Dobunni tribe and overlooking a similar site at Brownsover, just across the Avon valley, held by the Coritani, the river forming the territorial boundary. In the light of current knowledge, these assumptions can no longer be accepted. The earthworks at Brownsover bore little resemblance to a hill-fort and were in fact the remains of a village which in the 14th century was one of the largest around Rugby. By the end of the 16th century, it had been emparked and reduced to a small hamlet and, in 1629, the park was further enlarged. The description by Bloxam of the remains in his day is typical of a shrunken and emparked village site, and is shown clearly on his own and Giffney's plans.

Many former ideas about the Iron Age in Britain have had to be rejected or revised radically in the wake of recent archaeological advances. Until the late Iron Age, in the first century B.C., the names of the tribal peoples living in this island are not known, and their boundaries of influence were never clearly defined. This central area of the Midlands does not appear as part of the territory of any identified tribe, but the Coritani (properly Corieltauvi) were to the north-east, the Catuvellauni to the south-east, the Dobunni to the south-west, and the Cornovii towards Chester on the north-west. The absence of a local tribe name does not, however, necessarily suggest that this region was unoccupied. There is firm evidence that there was an array of early settlements in this area from the line of the Fosse Way across the upper Avon valley to the Jurassic Ridge in Northamptonshire, shown in detail in Map 1. These began as farmsteads, possibly in the late Bronze Age, singly or in small groups, but in time economic, social and environmental factors reduced their numbers as they evolved into a network of villages spaced fairly evenly at 3-3½ miles (4.8-5.6 kilometres) apart, each having territory covering, on average, about six square miles.

Most of these emergent villages are located on hilltops or hillsides, a few at stream or river crossings. Their place-names have original and distinctive meanings describing their situations in the landscape, with the important feature that their roots are, entirely or in part, not Saxon or Roman but Celtic, which was the language spoken in these islands from the beginning of the Iron Age, about 500 B.C., or even earlier. This indicates that they were established and given Celtic names during that period, and are likely to have been in continuous occupation since. An early date in the Iron Age is suggested by the fact that the Romans, on their arrival, found an already well-established and, as Map 1 shows, comprehensive network of roads serving these villages, and others further afield.

Rugby was one such primary settlement, in a strategic position at a meeting of roads on a hilltop and overlooking a ford across the river Avon. The name 'Rugby' has come down to us through the medieval form 'Rokeby' from the Saxon 'Rocheberige', which appears in Domesday Book latinised as 'Rocheberia', the Saxon 'g' being silent. This in turn derives, not from the 'burgh' or an imaginary Briton called 'Hrocca', as has been suggested, but from the Celtic prefix *droche-*, meaning rough, wild or bad, added to *brig*, a height, top or summit. Thus we have 'Droche-brig', the rough and wild hilltop, a suitable description of its location. These two words are still used with little change in Irish and Scots Gaelic and in Welsh.

Amongst other names with Celtic origins are Crick, from *creik*, a crag or cliff, East and West Haddon, from *ard-dun* or *ardan*, a high hillside, and Elkington, a lost village which was 'Elteton' in Domesday, with the root *ilde-dun* meaning multiple hillsides, which describes very well the heavily-fissured ground known as 'the Hollows'. Others are half Celtic, half Saxon or Norse, and a few have more recent names where a Celtic name has been lost, perhaps due to a period of desertion.

Rugby owed its early evolution as a market town to its position at the focus of a network of important through-roads (see Map 1). Two main routes crossed and divided here: one ran east from a probable Iron-Age site at Barrs Hill, Coventry, with alternative routes out of Rugby towards Hunsbury, the hill-fort near Northampton; the other came southwards from Leicester to Oxford, forking at Rugby to follow divergent ways to Oxford, forming a 'Y' junction where the present clock tower stands. The area between the two arms became the site for a market-place, most of which remained an open space until the 17th century. The pattern of streets formed at this early stage has survived longer than any other feature of the town, but unhappily it is now under continual threat from the depredations of modern 'developers' and liable to be lost at any time.

No significant Roman remains have been found in Rugby, but they have been abundant in the vicinity of the Watling Street and the sites of Tripontium and Bannaventa, and also near Princethorpe on the Fosse Way, which was an old road taken over and built up by the Romans for army use. The Watling Street was one of the military routes cutting across the countryside and existing roads as intrusively as our motorways (see Map 1), with legionary depots along them at intervals rather like service-stations.

The traditional view of the Saxon invasions of this country in the fourth century as a succession of violent pillaging raids followed by forcible settlement with the virtual extinction of the native, mainly Celtic, population is no longer accepted. There certainly were sporadic raids from both east and west coasts, but by the middle of the fifth century the settlement movements proper had begun. Their general tenor was peaceful, made by slow infiltration over a long period, often in family groups, and helped perhaps by an already friendly continental element in the country. In time, of course, Saxon domination became complete, but it seems that the newcomers preferred at first to be independent rather than impose upon the existing order, for the sites chosen were nearly always on boundaries of old villages where land had probably been waste after the end of Roman rule.

They settled along existing roads in family farms, which evolved into typical long 'street' villages in the fashion of modern ribbon development, in marked contrast to the older compact forms.

Their names are Saxon in origin and so can be distinguished from those of the older Celtic villages. Farm names were the most common, such as *-tun*, *-ham*, *-worth* and *-cote*, or boundary marks such as stone, brook, a tree name or simply 'tree' itself, often coupled with a personal Saxon name. In addition, there is a later class of name introduced by Norse settlers using Scandinavian words. Most primary villages eventually came to have two or perhaps three Saxon or Danish satellites situated on their borders, although almost certainly many others did not survive. Rugby is encircled by as many as six, all with Saxon names – Clifton, Hulle and Moreton, Bilton, Long Lawford, Newbold, and Brownsover – all of which lie on its ancient borders in a circle about 1½-1¾ miles from the town. There may have been another in the gap between Bilton and Hillmorton, but no traces have been found. This attraction to Rugby could well have been due to its early success as a trading centre.

The effect on Rugby of the six satellites was to produce a drastic contraction in the area of its three open fields and distortion of their shape, clearly seen in Map 4. Suthbroke Field on the west was reduced to a long, narrow strip, and the town was no longer at the centre of its open fields. By this time, the open-field system must already have become established, which could hardly have been after the late seventh century, and was perhaps as early as the fifth. The same happened at Barby, an abandoned Iron-Age site resettled by Danes, when the new village of Kilsby was set up on its border cutting the East field of Barby down to a narrow strip. It is an irony of history that the present borough of Rugby extends almost to its old Iron-Age limits.

Market-places where local people regularly gathered for trade and business were the most effective places for the Christian missionaries to preach the Gospel, and where it was their practice to set up a tall wooden preaching cross. Once they had converted the thegn who was lord of the manor, his tenants were likely to follow suit. It is now recognised that many of the first churches were the property of manorial lords, built on demesne land, usually not far from the Cross and convenient to the Hall or manor house. The lord then endowed his church with land and income for the support of a priest nominated either by himself or by a monastic community. Although many churches were first built of timber for speed unless stone was plentiful, permanent stone buildings eventually replaced them.

Once a church was established, the cross was often retained in the churchyard as a Christian symbol and rebuilt in stone. Having lost its primary role, it became associated with the market and was a familiar sight in the market-place. This dual tradition persisted long afterwards, instances of trading in the churchyard being common in the Middle Ages, and the market cross was used for preaching by friars in the 13th and 14th centuries, by the Tudor Puritans and, most notably, by John Wesley in the 18th century. In Rugby, an important discovery of the middle section of an eighth-century cross-shaft built into a wall of St Andrew's Church was made during rebuilding in 1877. It is made of locally-available hard Keuper gritstone, and is evidence of a Saxon church in Rugby.

The Rugby market cross stood on the site of the present Clock Tower at least into the 16th century at what was known appropriately as the Crossing. The church is only a short distance away, as would be expected, yet the early Hall was also close at hand. This has not hitherto been recognised. South of the church in the grounds of the old Rectory, now a marriage guidance centre, was a moated enclosure of about three-quarters

2a., b. & c. This section of the shaft of a late eighth-century cross is unique in this part of the Midlands. It is about 18 ins. (46 cm.) high, with three surviving carved faces, the fourth having been broken away. It was discovered in the wall of St Andrew's Church during an demolition in 1877, and found its way into a garden in Horton Crescent. In 1919 it was presented to Rugby School Museum, transferred to the Rugby Library and Museum in 1938, and is now on display at the County Museum at Warwick.

a. The front face shows a figure displaying an open book to the onlooker. There was clearly a panel above, and the head of what may have been an angel appears below.

b. The left side depicts a long-necked bird perched in a conventional vine scroll.

c. The right side is carved with vine-scrolls issuing from a cornucopia carrying a central bunch of fruit, similar to that on the Bakewell cross in Derbyshire.

of an acre and still visible up to the 17th century. It then enclosed the parsonage, but all traces disappeared when the present house was built. The only sufficiently important place in a village to be protected by a moat, except where there was a castle, was the Hall or manor house. It was exceptional for the house of a parson to be moated, unless perhaps a bishop held it as part of his manorial estate, and as Rugby was a lay manor, this site could only have been the early moated Hall before it was taken over for the first Rector's house.

Where the patronage of a church belonged to the lord of the manor and his successors it did not necessarily go with the manorial estate. In the time of Edward the Confessor, Alwyn the Sheriff (of Warwickshire) appears to have passed many of his estates, including Rugby, to his more famous son Thurkill of Warwick. Alwyn retained the manor of Clifton with his church there, but in Rugby the church 'went with him' instead of to his son, and he provided a chaplain for Rugby from Clifton. In 1143 both churches, as well as Brownsover, were assigned to the abbey of St Mary de Pratis in Leicester, and only after litigation in 1200, confirmed in 1220, was the then lord of the manor, Henry II, son of Henry I de Rokeby, able to recover the patronage and the right to present a priest as Rector to Rugby.

When soon afterwards the first Rector was appointed, a house was needed for him near the church. It is probable that the Hall was consequently moved to a new moated site north of the church at the lower end of today's Regent Street, and a Rectory House built in its place. There are several similar instances known and confirmed in North-amptonshire, so that Rugby is not an isolated example. Pipewell Abbey had a grange at Nepland but, also early in the 13th century, it was moved elsewhere on the Abbey's estate where Rugby School now stands, and indeed it is quite possible that the vacated grange site was taken over for the Hall by an arrangement with the Abbot. The grange would not have occupied the rectory site originally as was once suggested, for that area was too restricted and close to the town and, moreover, it was not until late in the 13th century that monastic granges began to be defended by earthworks of any kind.

Nothing remains of a Norman church, and only a complete excavation would reveal any evidence for its existence. However, it is known that soon after A.D. 1200, Henry II de Rokeby rebuilt the chancel, probably in the current Transitional Norman style and, as the nave was not altered, it must have been of stone matching the new chancel. Thus, at an early date, Rugby had a stone-built church which was probably Saxon in origin.

Soon after the Conquest, hundreds of motte-and-bailey castles were rapidly thrown up in a network carefully planned by the barony to deal with uprisings, which in the Midlands took place between 1068 and 1070. Such a castle was built at Rugby as part of a local network, later in the control of the Earls of Leicester, near to the Leicester Road crossing of the Avon, a typical position and in the right place relative to the neighbouring castles. The site has been completely obliterated by modern industry, with little hope of finding any trace of its existence.

The medieval town grew out of the early village, changing in response to social and economic pressures, yet remaining clustered around the Crossing, as Map 3 shows. The road from Barby, known as 'Fielden Street', entered the town along the line of Little Church Street, or Old Town Street as it was once called. Originally it curved gently at the lower end past the church to the Cross, but the graveyard was extended westwards, possibly when the nave of the church was rebuilt and the tower added in about 1350, the road being diverted sharply to the west on a course which has not been altered since. By the 17th century, however, the rear premises of buildings facing the cross, including the

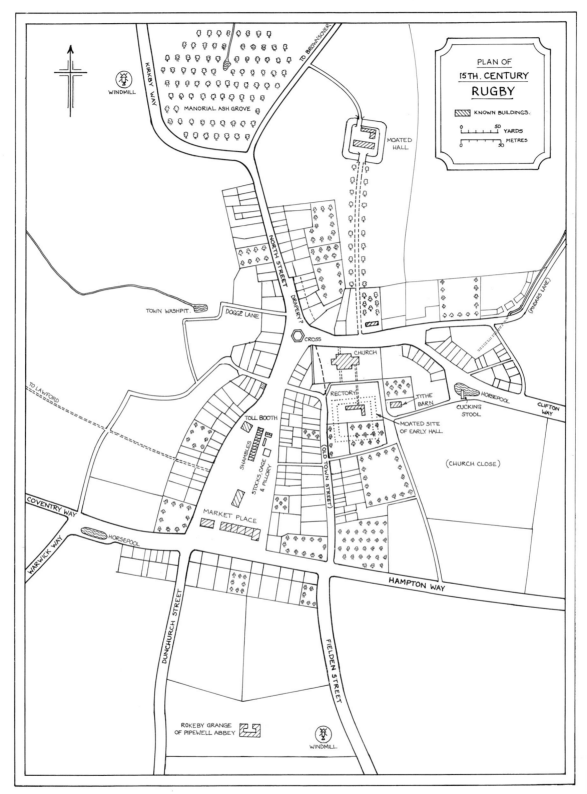

3. Plan of 15th-century Rugby. The street layout of the town has changed little from medieval days, except for the infilling of the market-place, and is still recognisable. Dogge Lane, which became Windmill Lane in the 19th century, has now gone, and the ash copse is survived by a small clump of trees in Caldecott Park.

George Inn, had encroached over the graves up to the line of the old road, and in the 19th century quite a number were disturbed during building work.

Dunchurch Street formed the other arm of the 'Y' junction on the west side of the market-place where Drury Lane now runs, but its path to the Cross is now interrupted at the lower end by intrusive buildings first erected in the 17th century and later rebuilt. Hampton Way crossed the south side of the market-place, but it appears that by the 17th century the straight course of the road had been diverted by the obtrusion of buildings from the site of Rugby School.

The whole market-place triangle was open, with adequate space for the penning of different kinds of livestock. The survival in many market towns of names such as Sheep Street, Swine Street, and Butchers Row shows that each class of animal had its traditional area. On both sides of the market-place were houses with shop-fronts where dairy produce and food would be sold. The Crossing area contained more shops including the Drapery, with mercers, ironmongers, chandlers, cordwainers and other tradesmen, and an abundance of inns and ale-houses. Along the sides of the market-place on market days were stalls, temporary at first, which in time became fixtures and the start of a growing row of more permanent shops. In this way the eastern edge of the market-place was first built up, probably in the late 13th century, to form what is now Little Church Street and at the same time effectively reducing the open space for livestock.

By the 14th century the row of stalls known as the Shambles had become a permanent line of shops in the centre of the market-place, where they have remained ever since. The name, from the Latin *scamellum*, a small stool or bench, came to refer to a market-stall, especially where meat of any kind was prepared and sold. They were 12 single-storied shops, half-timbered with mud-and-wattle infilling and thatched with straw and, due to this form of construction, needed frequent repair and periodic rebuilding. Behind them lay the slaughter-yards, and nearby were the stocks, pillory and the cage or lock-up, in perhaps the most noisome place possible. It could hardly have been more unpleasant for the officer whose duty it was to stand guard over any malefactor! The tumbrel, or cucking-stool, for the punishment of women brewers who broke the Assize of Ale and also for scolds and troublemakers, was by the horsepool on the eastern side of town, opposite the present *Squirrel Inn*.

Halfway between the end of the Shambles and the west side of the market-place was the Toll-booth or Market Hall, where market dues were collected and trading standards upheld, and where generations of the Harper family were tollmen. This was located near the present Co-op butchers' premises, at one time the *White Hart Inn*. Across the south end of the market-place were a few buildings, barns and stables, with an inn known as the *Red Lion* on the western corner of what is now Sheep Street. Until the 16th century, there were altogether some 20 shops and between 13 and 20 stalls in the market-place, besides the Shambles, and a further 14 shops and 15 stalls around the Crossing and in adjacent streets.

Rugby was then a spacious town with a fair number of roomy houses of the 'open hall' type, half-timbered and thatched, with crofts and gardens, and space enough for others to be built within the town in the 15th century, whilst the humbler cottages known from repair accounts seem to have been of a better quality than the hovels so often pictured. If the 'great rebuilding' phase of the mid-16th century affected Rugby, adding first floors to the open halls and inserting chimney-stacks in place of open hearths, no signs have survived, but new stone houses made their appearance by the middle of the 17th century, and a few still remain.

The prosperity of medieval Rugby was due mainly to its position as a market town and trading centre, agriculture being less important partly because its area of open fields had been much reduced by the encircling villages. Besides the usual market-town traders and craftsmen, many inhabitants were engaged in the active cloth industry which grew up in the wake of the trade which developed in Coventry in the 13th century. However, this local manufacture in Rugby and other towns contributed to the ultimate decline of Coventry as a cloth-making centre by the 15th century. The mill by the Avon was used for fulling, with tenters' yards for drying and stretching the cloth near at hand, whilst the finished fabric was probably sold mainly at the Drapery in the market-place.

Although there was legislation to control markets and trading in the earliest laws of the Saxon kings – in which it is implicit that such markets were customary everywhere – it was only late in the 12th century that strict legislation began. The great upsurge in the economy of that time created growing trading activity and the need for new markets, and the Crown intervened to regulate trade and standards and to exploit it for revenue. All new weekly markets could be held only by virtue of a royal licence granted to the lord of the manor for a usual fee of five marks, and in return he was entitled to the profits of the market through rents, tolls and stallages. Such licences were also purchased by the lords of long-established market towns, as Roger de Camville did before 1200 for the Sunday market at his manor of Lilbourne, but it was not until 1255 that Henry II de Rokeby bought the franchise of his Saturday market in Rugby as well as a fair for three days in August. Neighbouring new markets were licensed at Daventry (Wednesdays) by 1200, and Lutterworth (Mondays) in 1214, whilst in 1265 Thomas de Astley was granted one on Saturdays at Hillmorton, changed to Wednesdays three years later to avoid clashing with Rugby, and then to Tuesdays in 1334 because of rivalry with Daventry.

By the mid-14th century trade was declining, owing to land shortages, famines and a succession of plagues. There is no data from which to assess the impact on Rugby of the Black Death, but where records survive for nearby villages, they show a drop in population of 20-40 per cent between 1327 and 1381. Market towns suffered a fall in trade, many smaller markets having to close, and recovery was slow. Rugby's chief rivals were Lutterworth and Daventry, and it is significant that, in 1472, freedom from tolls at Rugby were granted to the men of Fawsley hundred to entice trade away from Daventry, which lay in that hundred.

Although Rugby continued to thrive, the reduced livestock business used less market space, leaving more scope for building. This had begun southwards from the Shambles in the 16th century, eventually forming the present High Street. Until the 18th century the west side remained open, but it was then filled in from the Toll-booth as far as the *Red Lion Inn* to form Sheep Street on the east and Stockwell Lane, now Drury Lane, on the west. Some new buildings were commercial premises, but most were private houses.

The land where Rugby School now stands was once part of a 200-acre estate granted by Henry I de Rokeby to the Cistercian abbey of Pipewell, near Corby in Northamptonshire. The grange was moved there in the 13th century from its old Nepland site, and a windmill erected adjacent to Fielden Street – its mound or 'tump' is now the 'Island'. The estate, with the Abbot as lord of the manor, had its own manorial rights and was distinct from the town manor and market, which had passed from the descendants of Henry II de Rokeby to the Earls of Stafford in 1350. As the Cistercians administered their estates from the central monastery, there was no seigniorial hall in Rugby, and their manorial courts were held at the grange. It was only at the end of the 17th century that the two manors were combined by the Burnaby family who built a new manor-house on the grange site.

There is here a remarkable historical irony, and a certain justice for Lawrence Sheriff, founder of the School. On the grange estate was a row of nine houses with crofts, facing north towards the market-place, and standing back from the street once known as School Street but now Lawrence Sheriff Street. At the beginning of the 16th century, two free tenants, the brothers Edmund and William Shrife (Schrieff, Sheriff), each leased a messuage from the abbot, and this William was the father of Laurence Sheriff who was born there in 1515 or 1516. William was a chapman dealing in spices, and a grazier with land in Rugby and Hillmorton – a man of fair means. He was assessed in the 1524 subsidy on his moveable goods at £4, an average figure, whilst at his death in 1540 the value of his inventory was put at the appreciable sum of £54 10s. Unfortunately, his will is lost, but the Probate Act names his son Laurence Sheryff as heir and executor.

Laurence followed his father as a grocer in spices, was apprenticed to William Walcott in London, and a year after his father's death obtained the Freedom of the Grocers' Company, being elected to its Livery in 1554 and made Second Warden in 1566. In the meantime, in 1559, he received a grant of arms which have since been adopted by the School. In common with many successful merchants of the time, he invested his profits widely in property, which included Conduit Close in London, Brownsover parsonage and glebe land, and a piece of land in Rugby opposite St Andrew's Church. He died in 1567, and by his will provided for the foundation of a free grammar school for the children of Rugby and Brownsover and lodgings for four poor men, to be financed out of the income from Brownsover and Conduit Close, with bequests for building a schoolhouse and almshouses on his property opposite the church in Rugby. The four almsmen were soon lodged in part of the 'mansion-house' he had already built there, but the school opening was delayed until the schoolhouse was finished in 1574. After only a few years, it entered a long period of trouble and litigation which lasted until 1667, arising in the first place out of inadequate trust provisions and dishonesty and laxity among the trustees, when its very existence was threatened. However, in that year the Board of Trustees was able to take matters in hand, and with an assured income the school began to grow steadily. The old premises became overcrowded and, before long, too dilapidated for repair. After abandoning proposals made in 1742 to enlarge the existing site, the old Pipewell grange property was bought for the school, which moved in 1750 to occupy the very place where its founder was born and brought up!

It is not easy, without extensive guesswork, to arrive at a reliable figure of population for any year, including Domesday, until the first census of 1801, owing to shortcomings in the records. However, the number of houses can be ascertained for Rugby with fair accuracy in three instances. The Bishops' Returns to the Privy Council in 1563 give the number of 'howseholdes' belonging to the 'Churche of Rokeby' as 69, which may be valid if households can be equated with houses, yet as only members of the Church of England were counted, recusant Catholics and Dissenters were not included, and the figure is undoubtedly on the low side. The Hearth Tax returns of 1662 to 1674 are more reliable, although they vary from year to year. The best figures are for 1672, when 183 houses were recorded, made up of 143 houses and 40 'poore cottages that stand on the Common', which tallies with the number given by Rev. William Thomas for 1728/9 of 'about nine score and three' houses in his 1730 edition of Dugdale's *Antiquities of Warwickshire*. The population appears to have at least doubled in the hundred years after 1563.

The medieval system of land tillage exerted a stranglehold over any expansion of the town. The tenants of the manor shared the arable land of the open fields in interspersed

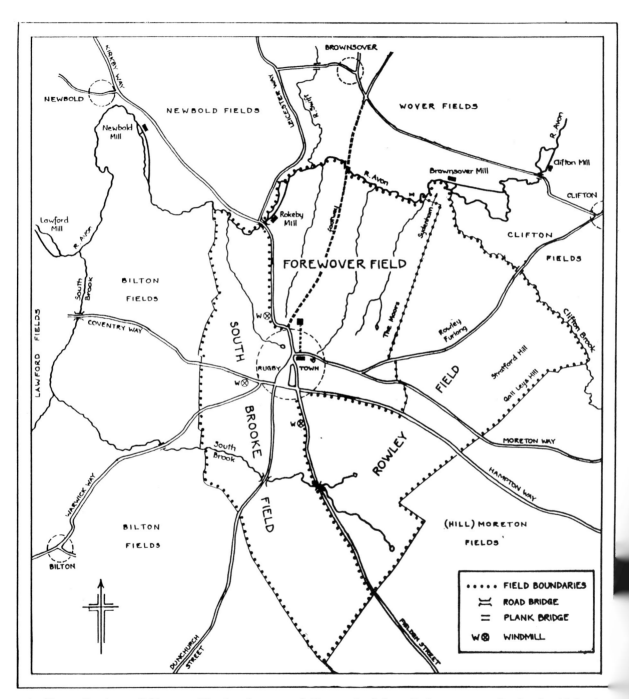

NEWBOLD

KIRKBY WAY

NEWBOLD FIELDS

BROWNSOVER

WOVER FIELDS

Newbold Mill

LEICESTER WAY

R. Swift

R. Avon

Clifton Mill

Lawford Mill

R. Avon

Brownsover Mill

R. Avon

CLIFTON

FOREWOVER FIELD

CLIFTON FIELDS

SOUTH BROOK

BILTON FIELDS

Rokeby Mill

Footway

The Moors

Sydenham

Rowley Furlong

Clifton Brook

COVENTRY WAY

W ⊗

W ⊗

RUGBY TOWN

Swotford Hill

ROWLEY FIELD

Goil Leys Hill

South Brook

W ⊗

MORETON WAY

SOUTH BROOKE FIELD

HAMPTON WAY

(HILL) MORETON FIELDS

BILTON

BILTON FIELDS

WARWICK WAY

DUNCHURCH STREET

FIELDEN STREET

····· FIELD BOUNDARIES
⋈ ROAD BRIDGE
= PLANK BRIDGE
W ⊗ WINDMILL

4.   The medieval open-field system. The three large open fields contained about 42 virgates, or yardlands, of arable land, nominally about 1,600 acres, of which 2½ virgates were glebe land. Their shapes reflect the effect of the encroachments made by the encircling Saxon villages. The map shows the location of a few of the many named furlongs. The surprising number of water-mills along the Avon suggests that the river ran deeper and faster than it does today.

strips, amongst which was often distributed likewise the demesne land held by the lord himself, so little was readily available for building except by common agreement. Once any waste land or old closes had been built on, the only option to cope with an expanding population was to crowd more houses within the confines of the town. Enclosure provided the chance to ease the problem when the open fields were shared in self-contained plots by individual owners or tenants, who might then be persuaded to sell land for housing.

In view of its importance as a trading centre, Rugby was a modest size at that time, especially in comparison with Daventry which was half as big again, with 292 houses. After the Enclosure Award of 1774 was implemented, expansion outside the town became possible, yet landlords appear to have been reluctant to sell any land for housing, which may account for the absence of late 18th-century development on the outskirts of Rugby. The relentless rise in poulation put considerable pressure on space in the town, where the ever-present danger of fire was becoming critical by the 18th century, serious outbreaks occurring in 1716 and 1738. The old timber-framed houses were gradually either refaced with brick and given tiled or slated roofs, or rebuilt in brick as it became more readily available. Windmills were particularly prone to destruction by fire, the eventual fate of all five in Rugby, while public houses seem to have been more than commonly liable to the same danger.

Market towns at crossroads, such as Rugby, always had problems with homeless itinerants and beggars, who lost their traditional Church support at the Reformation. The successive Elizabethan poor laws laid the onus of their care on the parishes, to be administered by the Overseers of the Poor, and paid for by tax levies on each parish. The European wars of the 18th century added discharged soldiers and sailors to the tally of wayfarers, as the Rugby Constables' Accounts show. In the interests of hygiene, the Overseers built a public bath house in 1764 over a spring-head in Bath Lane, now Bath Street, where it was in use for the next 50 years. In an effort to cope with rising costs and to alleviate poverty, Rugby combined with ten neighbouring parishes in 1818 to form a Poor Law Union, and provided a new workhouse for 130 inmates at the eastern edge of the town on Lower Hillmorton Road. It was never much more than half full because of its severe regime, but costs were halved within two years! At present, it is used by the Hospital of St Cross as an extension.

By the early years of the 19th century, overcrowding in the town was rapidly making some areas unsanitary and unfit to live in. The air was foul, fever and disease were rife, and a severe cholera epidemic broke out in 1832. Courts were chronic blackspots, where families shared one privy, sewage ran into open cess-pits or surface drains, and drinking water was often contaminated. The same conditions were only too common in other Midland towns, and improvements were desperately needed. The passing of the Public Health Act in July 1848 brought an immediate response in Rugby, leading to a Local Board of Health being formed in September 1849, the third in the country after Coventry and Croydon. Efforts immediately began to provide a supply of fresh water to the town from a water-tower built on the high ground to the south, on Barby Road, and it was only after several abortive attempts that an adequate source of clean water was found in the river Avon. In 1865, the water-works were opened, yet it was not until 1876 that there was a continuous supply. Sewage and drainage were dealt with more quickly, and by 1854 almost four-fifths of the town had been connected to the filter beds by the river at Newbold, although it took another ten years for the work to be completed.

Another increasing hazard came from the livestock markets and horse fairs in the town, which had to be closed to traffic. In May 1850, the market franchise was transferred by the lord of the manor, Thomas Caldecott, to the Board of Health, which took a lease on a piece of glebe land east of Trinity Church known as Reynolds Field or the Cricket Field, and the livestock business moved there in 1870. They later bought Stanleys Field on Hillmorton Rad as a permanent site, but because of powerful objections from nearby residents, a location was eventually obtained near to the railway station and opened in 1877, leaving Stanleys Field to become what is now the Recreation Ground.

The Industrial Revolution left Rugby untouched directly, until the Oxford canal was opened from Coventry as far as Hillmorton in 1773, and completed to Oxford in 1790. It ran clear of the town itself along the 325ft. contour, but there were wharves within easy reach to ship bulk cargoes such as coal, building materials and grain. The first turnpike road into Warwickshire came to Dunchurch in 1703 from Stony Stratford, which was linked to London, and extended later to Birmingham and Holyhead. The earliest from Rugby was to Lutterworth in 1785, continued to Dunchurch by 1826, with others to Market Harborough, Hinckley and Warwick, toll-gates being installed around the town. During the years before toll-roads came to Rugby, Dunchurch – a village a quarter of its size – was the nearest posting stage to London, and it was for this reason that mail was directed to 'Rugby near Dunchurch'. The advent of the railways dealt a death-blow to the turnpike trusts, and the last in the county expired in 1885.

A profound change came when the London to Birmingham railway opened in 1838 with a station at Rugby, albeit away from the town centre. Two years later, the Midland Counties Railway brought its line to the town, mainly for coal freight, and the station had to be moved further east. Within ten years four other companies followed, making Rugby a major junction, and when the Northampton loop-line arrived in 1882, the station was rebuilt another 100 yards eastwards on its present site. The substantial increase in trade, not only in freight but also in livestock, was so beneficial to the market that Rugby began to recover its former dominance. The railways first brought their own industry and a maintenance depot, then in 1892 introduced heavy engineering with a locomotive erecting shop, followed by the wagon works of Thomas Hunter. The final domination of the town by engineering came when the firm of Willans and Robinson opened their electrical works in 1899, and the British Thomson-Houston Company opened for production in 1901. For the next 50 years, the two firms and the railway companies provided the bulk of employment until after the Second World War, when a change in the industrial climate brought new and more diverse opportunities for the long-term benefit of the town.

The transformation of a country market town into a railway and industrial centre, with a prospering public school, made improvements to its public image and facilities an urgent necessity. Paving the streets and footways in the centre of the town started in 1835, but not until the turn of the century were the main roads all finally macadamised. The streets were lit after a private company was formed in 1838 to supply the town with gas, which was gradually laid on for all public buildings and homes. It had no rival for 60 years until an Electric Light Committee was set up in 1900 and commissioned the British Thomson-Houston Company to generate electricity for the town. It was switched on in 1902, and used to light the Clock Tower in 1904, but the streets remained gas-lit until the 1930s.

The demands on housing, already increasing by the end of the 18th century, rose very sharply after the coming of the railways, although the companies provided for many of their staff. The first new building began west and south of the town in about 1830, using a distinctive yellow/grey local brick of good quality, which was later employed for some rebuilding in the town centre. The number of houses increased by 50 per cent in the decade from 1831 (496) to 1841 (759), taking up over 30 acres of land, to reach a peak in the following ten years. The real development of the town, however, was initiated in 1866 by the formation of the Rugby Freehold Land Society, later to become the Rugby Building Society, which set out to purchase land for sale as building lots to its members. Their first acquisition was off Victoria Street in New Bilton in that year, and followed in other areas until 1922, when the Paddox/Ashlawn Road estates were begun. By 1927 the Society had changed its policies, after having made a unique contribution to the growth of the town. Since then, development has continued in a much more piecemeal fashion, with as yet no end in sight.

With such a long history, it is regrettable that more has not been preserved, to be appreciated not only today but in the future. Rugby, although incorporated as a borough in 1932, is still in essence a small town with a recognisable character, albeit one which has changed from one century to another. However, unless there is a greater and more effective historical awareness, the town could lose itself in the tide of urban nonentity imposed by the property developers who are making one town indistinguishable from any other, and with scant regard for history.

A drawing after a sketch of cottages at the corner of Bilton Road and Lawford Road by Edward Pretty in 1847. By 1850 new houses had taken their place which can be seen in Plate 74.

The Plates

Market Place

5. An exceptional picture of the old *George Inn* about 1810, painted on glass once in Bennfield House, North Street. The inn was built for Thomas and Joyce Langley on their marriage in 1652, commemorated by a relief carving on a mantel beam of their initials, a heraldic shield, and the date, mis-read on its discovery as 1662. The Langley family lived there until 1770, to be followed in 1808 by the Butlin and Benn dynasty. Until 1840 two rooms were taken over by William Butlin for his bank, accessible from his shop next door on the right. The two cottages on the left became part of the inn at an early stage, the nearer already an ale-house.

6. The *George Hotel* dominating the east side of Market Place in 1876. The old inn was demolished in 1846, when the carved mantel beam came to light, and many of the materials were used in the new hotel. This closed in 1951 and, with the other premises on that side, was demolished in 1953 for a block of shops. The draper's shop on the right, once held by William Butlin, changed hands to Gibbs and Baker in the year of this picture, and to John Gibbs the following year.

7. A busy market day in about 1905, with traditional stalls round the Clock Tower. Permanent stalls have now been set up in the Gas Street area. The ground floor of Boughton House, behind the Clock Tower, was in use as Webb's clothes shop by 1902. The almshouses can be seen to the right.

8.   A quiet day in Market Place, *c*.1900. On the extreme left is the *Eagle Hotel*, a large inn of 18th-century origin which stretched back as far as the bend in Chapel Street. The original façade remains on the upper storey. In 1868 it was sold to the Wesleyan Methodist church, who turned it into a temperance hotel and built a new chapel alongside and converted the stables into schoolrooms. Next door was a bookshop, once Billington and Lawrence then George Over, which was built in 1801 on the site of *The Bear and Ragged Staff*, a half-timbered and thatched medieval inn named after the badge of the Earls of Warwick. The last landlord, from *c*.1772, Joseph Richardson, closed it in 1801 following the death of his wife.

9.   Before 1890 photographers relied upon heavy plate cameras and tripods. After this date, lighter, hand-held cameras became available, but still taking only glass plates. In 1895 the Kodak pocket camera appeared, with a fast roll film giving 12 negatives, thus making 'snapshots' possible. From this year a keen photographer, possibly from the Birmingham Society, toured Rugby, and a number of his negatives have survived. This 'snapshot', taken from the doorway of the *George Hotel*, was just in time to show the wicker pannier toppling from the tail of the fishmonger's cart.

10. This charming picture of two ladies crossing Market Place in 1895 is one of the best from our roving photographer – an early example of the art of the 'candid camera'!

11. A once familiar sight, even in the 1930s, was the street-piano (mistakenly called a 'barrel organ'), seen here in Market Place in 1896. Usually operated by Italians, often with the added attraction of a parrot or monkey, their number of tunes was limited, and they rarely stayed long in one place.

12.   The yellow fly, which was always ready outside the *George Hotel*, in 1896. In the background can be seen the post office on Chapel Street corner and the newly-rebuilt premises of Brown's fishmongers and Bennett's the hairdressers on the near corner.

13. Market Place between Chapel Street and the Wesleyan Chapel as it was in the 1880s. The house on the right, occupied by W. Smith, shoemaker, and W. Brown, fishmonger, was a roomy late 17th-century building, much modfied over the years. Thomas Bennett occupied the adjoining shop, taking over Brown's in 1892, Brown moving next door into the shoemaker's. The house was pulled down in 1894 and rebuilt as it is today. The post office stood on the corner of Chapel Street until 1901, when it was transferred to Albert Street.

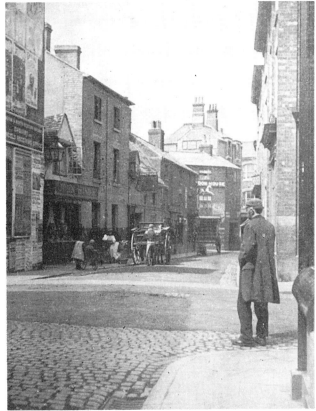

.   The corner of Chapel Street and Market Place in 94. In the 18th century this part of Chapel Street was led Lagoe's Lane (leading to Lagoe Place), becoming an Street in the 19th century. Drury Lane emerges on left to the side of a small shop with a gabled dormer dow, reputed to be the oldest house in Rugby, hough due to piecemeal rebuilding only the cob end l flanking Drury Lane is original. It was for many rs a butcher's shop, here in the hands of John Hinds, is now a charity shop.

15.   After an early attempt to form a co-operative society in about 1860 had failed, a printer, J. W. Kenning, succeeded in 1862, operating from the *Eagle Hotel* until a shop opened in North Street. In 1870 the society set up business at 45 Chapel Street next to the *Australian Arms*, this photograph of 1910 showing how much it had prospered.

North Street

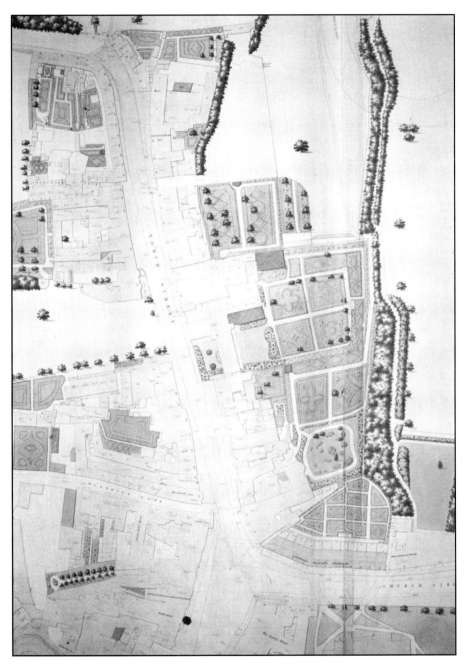

16. The Beatty Survey of the North Street area. As a consequence of the Health and Towns Act of 1848, surveys of six towns in Warwickshire were begun by the Ordnance Survey Department on a large 1:528 scale (ten feet to a mile). The work was carried out by a field detachment under Capt. Andrew Beatty R.E. The survey of Rugby, the first in the country to be issued, was begun in August 1850 and completed and issued in March 1851, followed by Coventry and Stratford in July. The cost charged to the town was £817 14s. 10d.

17. This photograph of the top of North Street can be dated precisely by the sale notices on the *Crown Inn* to Monday 2 November 1896, the day of the sale of its contents prior to demolition. It is the older of the two inns, being originally a late 17th-century house. The earliest landlord on record is John Sparrow (1789 to at least 1810), a hairdresser who continued to ply his trade in a wing of the house. It was pulled down shortly after the sale and replaced by the present building in 1897. The *Windmill Inn* next door was originally the late 18th-century Windmill House, so named because of its tall, narrow shape, home of John Allibone and then Robert Webb. It was first recorded as an inn in 1809, when Robert Barnwell was the landlord. Dogge Lane, between the two inns, became Windmill Lane by association with the house in the 1850s. The barber's shop below, run by A. Foxon, was replaced in 1903 by a brick and stone gateway into the *Windmill*'s yard. The next shop, a jeweller's, was the first premises of the Rugby Co-op from 1862-70 until their move to Chapel Street. All the buildings except the *Windmill Inn* have now gone.

18. The row of once well-known picturesque thatched cottages in North Street, *c.*1910. They were of a type widely built in the Midlands for over 200 years, and appear to date from the later years of the reign of Elizabeth I, the spaces between the timber framing originally having been filled with lath and plaster. In the early 18th century this was replaced with brick nogging, and the two cottages to the left were later completely rebuilt in brick, and chimney stacks added. In the late 1920s the cottages became derelict, one being used as a 'haunted house' during Rag Week. In June 1933, the roof of No.12 collapsed and the row was demolished. The whole site was acquired by Rugby Portland Cement Company for their Crown House offices and is now the National Westminster Bank.

19. A back view of No.11, the end cottage, in 1924 when it was occupied by William Brothers, a dairyman for over 2 years. From late in the 18th century the Shears family of blacksmiths lived here and in a neighbouring cottage, giving their name to the court of five houses behind the camera where at least two other members of the family had their smithies well into the 1840s.

20.   Boughton House, facing Market Place on the north-east side, was built in 1729 by Edward Boughton of Cawston for his daughter Judith on her marriage to her cousin Thomas Harris. In this photograph taken in 1888, the date and name of the house can be read over the fan-light within the porch, and the plate beside the side door carries the name of Harris and Son, solicitors, who used the upper floor. The house was sold in 1902 to Webb's, clothiers, who closed in 1953 when, in one of the worst examples of official vandalism, the house was demolished to make way for the present featureless row of shops.

21.   Boughton House decorated for the Golden Jubilee celebrations of 23 June 1887. In the doorway are Mr. and Mrs. C. F. Harris.

22.   This fine photograph, taken on whole-plate in 1888 of the drawing-room of Boughton House, is a valuable record of late Victorian furnishing and decoration in a well-to-do household of the period. On the sideboard, standing on a small easel, is the photograph reproduced above, and a number of other pictures in the room are easily recognised.

23. This splendid 17th-century building, known as Bennfield House, was destroyed in 1930 to make way for a post office. Built in 1669, probably for William Tilghman junior, it was rated at five hearths in 1670 and stood in extensive grounds, part of which were given over to a double-fronted house in the 18th century. In 1813, both houses came into the Benn family, and they lived and ran their businesses there until the last of the family, George Charles Benn, died in 1895. Note the 17th-century pillars and finials, repeated for the entrance to the field called Bennfield on the opposite side of the street.

24. A rear view of Bennfield House showing part of the extensive gardens and revealing the alterations made in the early 19th century, including a verandah and balcony.

25. The lower end of North Street decorated for the Diamond Jubilee of 1897. The date 1669 is clearly visible on Bennfield House, having been newly re-cut. Past the Georgian house are two brick pillars matching the other 17th-century pairs. The block of houses and shops further down was built on the site of an early workhouse after a new one was provided in Lower Hillmorton Road in 1818. The far cottage of the pair beyond the horse and cart was at one time a turnpike toll-house.

26. This double bow-fronted Regency house in North Street was built by Abraham Caldecott, and was for long the home of Thomas Bourne until, in 1865, it became the office of J. Ellis and Sons, coal-merchants. Over the porch lintel is carved 'Parkside House'. It disappeared in 1930 when the site was taken over by Hilton's Garage. This in turn came down in 1978 to provide a service entry to the Rugby Shopping Centre.

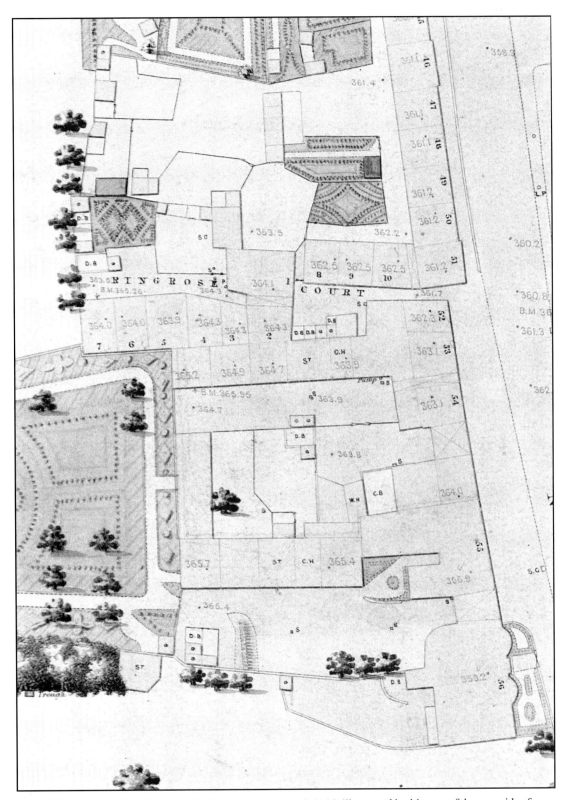

27.   The amount of detail included in the Beatty Survey of 1851 is illustrated in this map of the west side of North Street, opposite the *Saracen's Head*. Spot heights are given for each property, with the house-number in small figures. Abbreviations include St for stables, CH for coach house, and , for domestic details, CB for coal bin, DB for dustbin, S for a sink under a pump, and WH for wash-house. Privies are indicated by a small circle inside a square. The only departure from such accuracy is in the idealisation of the gardens. The house at the south-east corner is Parkside House, seen in plate 26.

28.   The lower west side of North Street, opposite the *Saracen's Head Inn*, decked out for the Diamond Jubilee of 1897. Behind the street frontage were a number of small, almost rural, courts, two being Ringrose Court and Jefferies Court. Thomas Collins was a butcher and the arched gateway below gave access for Beasley and Hands, coal merchants. All this property has been demolished, but the photograph may be compared with the map above (plate 27).

29.   A friendly call in a cottage garden near the town centre in a court behind the west side of North Street. Here was an area of countryside with gardens, orchard and fields leading back to Queen Street, all obliterated since the war by the Shopping Centre and car park.

30. The cottage shown here in 1902 was one of a pair at the bottom of North Street, demolished a year later to make way for Park Road, opened in 1904. In the late 18th century it was a toll-house on the road to Lutterworth, but when Abraham Caldecott built Rugby Lodge he acquired the cottages for his groom and shepherd, and the toll-bar was moved further out of town. The finger-board on the side of the cottage points to Newbold, six miles away, and Lutterworth, seven miles along a bridle path which still skirts Caldecott Park.

31. Rugby Lodge, seen here c.1895, stood where Holbrooke Avenue now rises off Park Road. Built by Abraham Cowley in 1801 when he became Lord of the Manor of Rugby, it probably replaced an earlier house built for William Caldecott and his wife Ann, a Boughton widow, who in 1748 were made custodians of the Manor and guardians during the minority of Anna Boughton. This explains why the new house, replacing the Burnaby manor house on the Pipewell estate sold to Rugby School in that year, was called the Lodge, rather than the Hall or Manor.

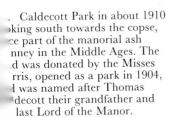

Caldecott Park in about 1910 looking south towards the copse, once part of the manorial ash ...nney in the Middle Ages. The ...d was donated by the Misses ...rris, opened as a park in 1904, ...d was named after Thomas ...decott their grandfather and last Lord of the Manor.

33. J. J. Webster, local carrier, with his Austin chain-drive, solid-wheeled van outside the Caldecott Park entrance. From 1904-36, like his father W. W. Webster before him, he plied the routes to Coventry and Warwick, working from Regent Street and living in Princes Street.

34. The *Avon Mill Inn* decorated for the 1897 Diamond Jubilee, with the landlord Francis Haynes, his family and staff. It stands on the site of the water-mill recorded in Domesday Book, and in use throughout the Middle Ages as a fulling-mill, with an adjacent horse-mill and 40 acres of land. The mill stones came from a quarry at Cathiron near Newbold, to be dressed at the mill. It was in the hands of the Bagshaws from Long Lawford by 1774, who sold out to the L.N.W.R. in 1855, when it became an inn, John Bagshaw having kept a beer-shop there as early as 1850.

Church Street

35.   The Lawrence Sheriff Almshouses in Church Street in 1900, looking west. They were numbered 1-12, from west to east, but in the photograph only Nos. 5-12 are visible. The original school stood on the site of Nos. 5-9, but after it moved in 1750 the first four of the new almshouses were built, now Nos. 9-12. In 1783 another four were added, Nos. 5-8, and finally in 1838, after much delay, the present Nos. 1-4 were completed. The other eight were then brought up to date and all were provided with porches. Sadly, they were demolished in 1961 and new almshouses opened in Warwick Street.

36.   View of Church Street *c.*1900 towards the Clock Tower. The building on the extreme right, once Butlin's Old Bank, became Lloyd's Bank in 1868, and was sold to the Midland in 1906. Moat House next door was demolished to make way for Regent Street in 1902 and, where the extension and the two nearest bays of the house once stood, the new Lloyd's Bank was built in 1906.

37. View of Castle Street from Church Street in 1901. The Regency house with arched Gothick doorways, Moat House, was built by W. F. Wratislaw before 1820. He lived and had his solicitor's business there until his death in 1853, when it was occupied by John Darby, a well-known horse-dealer. In 1879 premises behind were leased to Tattersall's, the London horse-dealers, to serve as their Midland branch. They built horse-boxes and conducted sales there until 1893, when they moved to larger premises at the bottom of Railway Terrace. The 18th-century house to the left was home to Richard Over for many years until the middle of the 19th century, and was replaced by shops on Regent Street corner in 1914.

38. No.17 Church Street, an unusual 18th-century brick house, drawn by J. H. Hollier in June 1867. Its frontage is almost identical to that of the *Windmill Inn* in North Street (see plate 17). This house was the home of James and Ann Richardson, but was sold to the National Provincial Bank in 1868 and demolished.

39. A 17th-century house in Church Street, now No.55 and occupied by Wilford Smith the chemists. The photograph, *c.*1900, reveals 18th- and early 19th-century alterations to its frontage and the addition of dormer windows. At that time, part of the building was a chemist's shop run by T. L. Pollock.

40.   Holy Trinity Church, built in 1854 to the designs of Sir Gilbert Scott as a chapel-at-ease to St Andrew's, boasted a notable organ-case and chancel screen by C. F. Bodley. A spire was intended, but the ground could not support the necessary foundations. In 1883 the tower showed signs of cracking for the same reason, and the north-west turret, seen here in an engraving of 1864, was taken down and the tower underpinned with concrete. The church went out of use and was demolished in 1983.

41. The north side of Church Street, opposite the *Lawrence Sheriff Arms*, in about 1865. The late 17th-century house on the right was divided between William Olorenshaw, a trader, and William Lucas, a butcher. His shop-front swung inwards to give access to the slaughter-yard at the rear. The building was replaced by a three-bayed house in 1872. The adjoining premises, the 'Thatched Cottage', contained the shops of Jonathan Gilbert, fishmonger, and Coleman's bootmakers, before demolition in 1875. The 18th-century brick cottage to the far right is the only survivor, but is unrecognisable as a medieval sham.

42. Church Street looking towards the town centre in 1878, the year that William Bowler was landlord of the *Lawrence Sheriff Arms*. The *Squirrel Inn* on the right, once three cottages, was first licensed by Fred Hillgrove in 1869. Opposite, Caldecott's, or St Andrew's girls' school, was opened in 1830 and extended to two storeys in 1888. It stood on the site of the old horsepool, a fact revealed when the foundations were being reinforced and which limited the height of the building.

Gas Street

43. This view from the top of Trinity Church tower in 1880 shows most of the Gas Street triangle, formerly known as Horsepool End. In the Middle Ages this area was a green or common, classified as the lord's manorial waste and entirely at his disposal. It was then called the 'Sarre Ground', meaning assarted or cleared ground. Some poor landless tenants of the manor were allowed small plots for their houses, paying a nominal annual ground rent to the lord of a peppercorn or, later, sixpence. Building was only allowed on part of the green, and in the mid-17th century there were only 40 houses. However, pressure of population caused that number to rise to more than 120 in the next 200 years. It became a slum area in parts, was mostly cleared by 1938, and is now used for markets.

44.   The Baptist Church was established in Rugby by Sir Egerton Leigh in about 1800, services being held in a cottage before a chapel was built in Gas Street in 1803, shown here before the enlargements of 1805 and 1859. Provision was made for a large Sunday School, and a graveyard was added as the burial space within the chapel became full. In 1906 a new church was built in Regent Street, and the old one sold to St Andrew's as a church hall. In 1935, with the building of Church House, the old chapel became home to the Rugby Brotherhood. Sadly, it is now due to be demolished for a shopping development.

45.   Care for the sick of Rugby began modestly in 1869 with the opening of a nursing home in Pennington Street, but the need for more space led to the purchase in 1876 of this building in Castle Street. It was erected in 1843 as a college for the deaf and dumb, and opened as a hospital in 1878, remaining in use until 1884 when the new Hospital of St Cross in Barby Road came into use.

46. This small 18th-century thatched cottage in Gas Street, originally No.18, was for a long time the home of a notable character, Thomas Grumble. One of a short row, it was typical of many crowded into the area. This picture dates from between 1895 and 1905, and evidence conflicts as to the identity of the woman and her neighbour. Since that time, most of this housing has been cleared, but this cottage was one of the last to go in the late 1930s.

47. Pinder's Lane, leading downhill from the north end of Castle Street, once contained a number of thatched cottages. In 1896 when this picture was taken, these, numbered 7-11, still remained at the top of the hill. They were built of brick with thatched roofs in the 18th century, and remained until the clearances of the 1930s.

Sheep Street

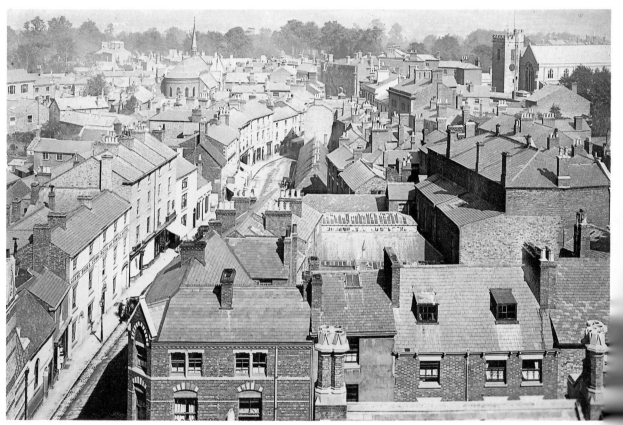

48.   A view of Sheep Street, *c.*1873, from the tower of Rugby School Chapel. The Wesleyan Chapel stands at the side of Market Place, and Boughton House can be seen in the centre as no clock tower obscured the view. St Andrew's Church appears with its new south aisle, before the rebuilding.

49.   The south end of Sheep Street in about 1910, when Taylor's the chemist's were on the east corner. Below Stannard's shop-front and wine vaults is the *Three Horseshoes Hotel* with James Loverock's drapery between. In the mid-1960s this shop, then F. G. Rainbow's, was incorporated into the hotel and rebuilt to conform with the rest of the 18th-century frontage. Note the style of doorway repeated from Stannard's to the far end of the hotel.

50.   The middle of Sheep Street looking north in 1895. Half way down on the right is the shop of Arthur J. Dukes, where groceries were sold from a counter to the left of the door and ironmongery on the right. The business began as Dukes and Bradshaw in 1886, but continued as Dukes from 1887 until 1956 when the building was replaced by a modern block. The name is remembered in Dukes' Jetty, which ran alongside the shop between the two streets.

51. View of Sheep Street from Dukes' yard, c.1880. The Shambles were still single-storied, the *Hen and Chickens* standing opposite on the Wooll Street corner, with Warwick House just below. The inn appears to be early 19th century, and although it was reputed to have been much older, the earliest recorded landlord was Ann Paybody or Pepperday in 1809. It was demolished in 1885 and rebuilt as the *Exchange Inn*, now called 'Olivers'.

52. Southward view of Sheep Street, c.1902. The Shambles, on the left, were rebuilt in 1830 after being sold by Thomas Caldecott, when they were officially known as the Manor Buildings. The two-storey section was added in 1890, but the shop-fronts have been considerably altered since. Opposite is the frontage of the Hands' shops, and beyond on the left is the rear of the old Town Hall buildings.

The Shambles.
.Sheep Street.

W.H.D. 1802.

53. An etching of the Shambles in 1802 when
they were a row of single-storey shops, said to be
of timber construction.

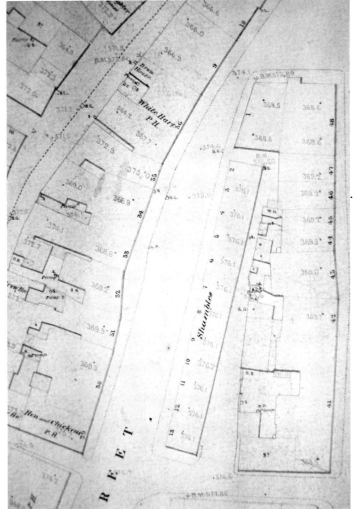

54. Part of Lower Sheep Street in the Beatty
Survey of 1850/1, the Shambles being numbered
-13. Opposite No.2 is the *White Hart Inn*, built
n the site of the medieval Toll-booth. The hotel
ad a yard and stabling behind in Drury Lane,
riginally Stockwell Lane.

55.   The stall of J. G. Sylvester at No.2 the Shambles in about 1888, with a display of poultry, fruit and oysters. The baskets hanging at the next stall belong to Albert Hall, and at No.4 is M. A. Green, clothier, followed by a butcher's stall – a typical mixture of trades.

56.   One of the best known of Rugby's family businesses was Sheasby's drapery and haberdashery, seen here in about 1905. They took over from Flintoff's at No.30, Warwick House, in 1896, where there had been drapers since 1850.

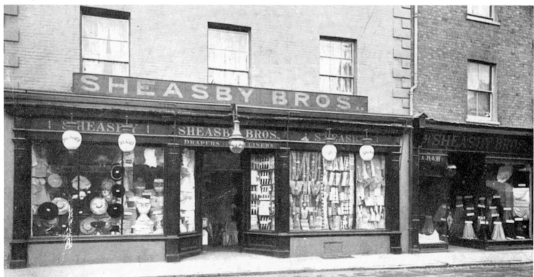

57.   A choice display of millinery in the shop of Mrs. Taverner at No.35 Sheep Street, seen with her husband, a draper, in 1890. They started business at No.19 Church Street in 1864, but a fire which started in Christmas decorations so damaged the shop that they moved to Sheep Street.

High Street

58.   The top of the High Street drawn in 1826 by Edward Pretty, looking toward the school entrance before the gateway was widened. To the right are the almshouses for six widows built and endowed before 1707 by Richard Elborowe (*c*.1625-1707), a native of Rugby and a successful London goldsmith. The school for 30 boys and girls was also endowed by him but became a National School in 1830 and in 1856, along with the almshouses, moved to Newbold Road to create space for a new town hall. Woolworths now stands on this site.

59.   This aquatint made in 1843 by C. W. Radcliffe is included for comparison with the reality of the engraving above (plate 58) and the photograph below (plate 62), as it has been so often used to illustrate the High Street as it then was. Clearly it is full of artistic licence, the street length being drastically curtailed so as to omit some buildings altogether, notably the Elborowe Almshouses. The left side is pure fantasy, showing the *Shoulder of Mutton* sign attached to a bow-windowed shop, and houses with jettied gables which never existed.

60. The Beatty Survey shows how the Elborowe School and Almshouses were located between High Street and Sheep Street, with entrances from each side. There was a paved play area, but the gardens behind the school building were not part of the property.

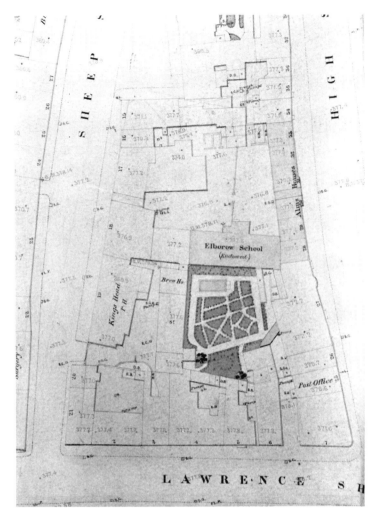

61. The first Town Hall was built in 1857 in place of the Elborowe School and Almshouses. It housed Council offices, Sessions Court-rooms, Assembly Room and Market Hall/ Corn Exchange. This engraving of 1864 shows the High Street façade in an imitation Palladian style. The offices moved to the new Benn Building in 1900, to be replaced by private businesses. Leon Vint's Picture Palace for 'Animated pictures and Vaudeville' – Rugby's first cinema – opened in 1911 on the enlarged first floor, again extended in 1919. In 1921 a fire damaged the building. Woolworths then took it over, and have since replaced it by a tasteless monolithic block, leaving only the 1919 extension of three bays, now over the Gas Showroom.

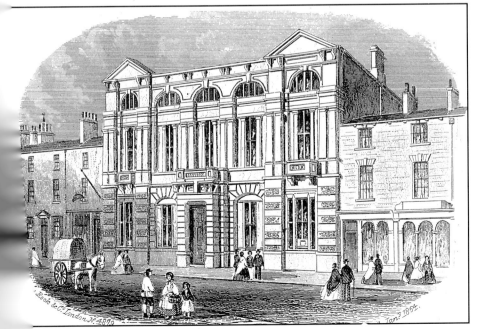

62.   View of Rugby School looking up High Street in 1890, with the Town Hall on the right. The buildings beyond are much as they appear in the 1864 engraving (plate 61). Note the method of supporting shop-awnings on poles in sockets at the edge of the pavement. Some of these holes survived into the inter-war period, and were often thought to have been cattle-pen stanchions.

63.   High Street in 1912. On the left is the Benn Building and opposite is Vint's booking office for the Palace Theatre in Railway Terrace. The poster is advertising the twice-nightly show featuring, among others, Wade and Lilian ('the Romany's Wooing') and Charlie Pix, scheduled to begin on Monday 10 June.

64.   The *Shoulder of Mutton* at No.4 High Street in 1896. A late 17th-century house, it was converted into an inn a century later, William Cave being the earliest recorded proprietor in 1795. The boarded-up shop to the left had been occupied by Henry Lander, chemist, for many years, but was being taken over by George Over for his bookshop. On the right of the picture were the premises of E. T. and W. J. Fell, cabinet makers.

65. The *Shoulder of Mutton* was demolished in 1898 to make way for new municipal buildings, opened in 1900, to replace the old Town Hall. George C. Benn bequeathed the inn to the service of the town in 1895, with generous provision for erecting and maintaining a new building for the benefit of the ratepayers. Comparison with plate 64 shows that the new Benn Building filled the site of the inn completely. In 1937 the council offices were transferred to larger premises at The Lawn in North Street and Marks and Spencer bought the Benn Building. The adjacent properties can still be recognised.

66. High Street in about 1912 looking towards the Clock Tower, with carriages waiting outside shops while their owners were inside. On the extreme right is the stylish front of the shop of George Dean, one of Rugby's most celebrated photographers.

Lawrence Sheriff Street

67. The corner of Sheep Street and School Street in 1851 by Edward Pretty, drawing master at Rugby School (1809-25) and later free-lance artist in Northampton. The corner house was No.21 Sheep Street, home of Henry Bromwich, a carrier. Below, at No.20, was Ebenezer Collins' barber shop. The sign of the 17th-century *King's Head* can be seen at roof level – the only surviving picture of this inn which closed in 1869.

68. Cottages at the corner of School Street, later Lawrence Sheriff Street, in the early 1860s. The corner house was occupied then by William Tomkinson, a greengrocer, with Luke Gibbons, a shoemaker, next door. They were demolished in 1868 when the present premises were built for James Symes, a tailor who moved from No.33 Sheep Street.

69. This engraving of School Street in 1865 shows the extent of alterations in this area. To the left of Read's the printers was James Wheeler, fishmonger, and under the sign of two cricket bats was the shop of Alfred Driver, self-styled 'Professor of Cricket' to the School. This shop combined with that of brazier William Porter next door to form the long-standing ironmongery business of Pratt and Sons.

70. The top of High Street with Pepperday's bookshop on the School Street corner. This drawing shows the narrowness of that street due to early encroachment by landowners on the school side. When the road was widened in 1929 the gabled south wing of Pepperday's was pulled down, leaving the north gable in place today. The drawing was made in 1885 just after New Big School was finished, by a sixth-former at the school, Charles A. Nicholson, later Sir Charles, Bart., F.R.I.B.A. and architect of the Memorial Chapel which was completed in 1923.

71. Elborowe's House (later Bucknill's), on the corner of Sheep Street and School Street, shown here in 1890 when James Brown, a wine merchant, was tenant. In 1645 Richard Elborowe senior from Yelvertoft bought the site of the old *Red Lion* and built in its place a large house with south-facing wings and extending between Sheep Street and Stockwell (Drury) Lane. This was the birthplace of Richard Elborowe, founder of the charity school and almshouses. It eventually passed to Rev. R. R. Bloxam in 1807. After his death in 1840 it was bought by a surgeon, Samuel Bucknill, who sold the western half to make way for a new *Red Lion* and wine store. The remaining half was refurbished with elaborate barge-boards on the gables, a heavy porch and considerable indoor alteration. The house and adjoining buildings were pulled down in 1926 and replaced by a new *Red Lion*, now the *Merry Minstrel* public house.

72. Elborowe's House soon after it was bought by Stannard's the wine merchants in 1896, and before the ground floor was converted into a shop in 1900. The wine-vault range was a surgery during the time of the Bucknills until James Brown leased it in 1861 for his wine store.

73.   The corner of Drury Lane and Lawrence Sheriff Street, *c*.1923, showing the wine store next to Elborowe's House which had become the *Red Lion Inn*. Drury Lane had by then become a service lane to the Sheep Street properties, but it originally formed the western edge of the open market-place. After being built up in the 18th century it was known as Stockwell Lane because of a well there. It was later nicknamed Tinkers Lane and in the 19th century received its modern name, allegedly from a London company of strolling players who lodged there.

Warwick Street and Bilton Road

74. An aerial view along Warwick Street from the tower of Rugby School Chapel, *c*.1880. Until 1820 most of the built up area to the right was garden, orchard and field. On the left, extending from the nearer Bilton Road corner to the head of Union Street opposite the west end of St Matthew's Church, was a long horsepool, often called Malin's Pool. On the far corner of Bilton Road is the house which stood where Sam Robbins first set up his garage and cycle shop, and the constricted entry into Lawford Road is apparent.

75. Warwick Street in about 1912 showing Addison Row, built in the 1840s, on the left with gardens in front which have now gone. Beyond is the church, built in 1841 in the popular Early English style to the designs of R. C. Hussey, but without the chancel which was added in 1914.

76. A busy scene in Warwick Street in about 1912, looking towards Rugby School. Previously known as Warwick Way or Road, it once extended along Bilton Road as far as the top of the hill by Westfield. The tower of the school chapel is one of Rugby's notable landmarks, designed by William Butterfield and built between 1872 and 1883.

77.   Until 1900 this mound stood just off Lawford Road, near the corner of Vicarage Road. Known as Butlin's Mound because of that family's ownership of the close where it lay, it was thought to have been a Bronze Age barrow, but excavation by A. E. Treen and examination during its destruction yielded only a deep layer of charcoal from burnt timber and some medieval pottery. This indicated that it was the tump of a post-mill, probably of the 14th century, which was destroyed by fire, a not uncommon fate. The illustration is from an 1888 painting by H. O. Richardson, a local artist.

78.   Oakfield House, off Bilton Road, was the family home of the Butlins until 1859. A year later the Rev. John M. Furness and his brother bought it as a preparatory school for boys, with a four-acre playing field. Originally there were only 14 pupils but numbers rose quickly so that by 1914, when this picture was taken, considerable extensions had been made to the house, which is the block on the right. In 1930 the school moved to Bilton and its name was changed to Longrood. Oakfield House then became a social clubhouse and underwent numerous alterations. The original late 18th-century house is presently being incorporated into a new office complex.

79. A 'candid snapshot' taken in 1896 of a lady cyclist passing the *Star Inn* in Warwick Street at the corner of Dunchurch Road. At this time cycling was becoming very popular, especially for ladies, and their machines were basically little different from those ridden today.

80. The shop on the corner of Bilton Road occupied in 1899 by Sam Robbins as a depot for the Diamond Cycle Manufacturing Company. He then opened the adjacent garage and in 1901 was claiming the ground in front of the cycle shop for himself. A year later he was again in trouble for obstructing the footpath with his cycles, and was summoned by the council. Today, the same premises remain a hindrance to traffic flow into Lawford Road.

81. Road repairs using a two-horse roller on Bilton Road in 1906. The creeper-covered house is The Hollies, and next door is St Matthew's Vicarage which was sold in 1969 and is now used as a Mencap hostel.

82. A watercolour made in 1838 by Edward Rudge of the view north from the bottom of Bilton Hill where the road crossed South (Sow) Brook, looking towards Christmas Hill which rises in front and to the right of the picture. The flat ground is at present part of Bernhard's Garden Centre, and Croop Hill estate lies over the skyline.

Clifton Road

RUGBY. CLIFTON ROAD.

83.   The once-familiar sight of cattle being driven along Clifton Road from Hillmorton, to turn right into Railway Terrace and the new cattle market, c.1903. Just past the turning is the two-storey Caldecott's Girls' School. Trinity Church stands on the left of the photograph. Two years earlier, Moutrie Road had been opened, the double-gabled Glebe House not yet obscured by the new house on the corner.

84. Two early Midland Red type FS buses, 'boneshakers' with slatted wooden seats, in Clifton Road outside Rainbow and Wadley's furniture shop in 1926. The leading bus served the Coventry and Leamington routes, carrying 34 passengers with driver and conductor. The triangular two-wheeled cart on the left carried a poster display which was pushed around town, rather like a sandwich board on wheels.

85. Clifton Road beyond Paradise Street looking east, c.1908. This is an example of the tree-planting carried out along selected roads leading into the town in 1886/7 in time for Victoria's Golden Jubilee. Such schemes had been tried twice before but failed because of vandalism. In 1886 the Rugby Town and Trade Association made a public appeal for subscriptions. The response was immediate, each tree with its guard being paid for by an individual at a cost of 10s. 6d. On both sides of Clifton Road 127 were planted, the first with due ceremony by Rev. C. Elsee next to Trinity Church, after which planting followed along Whitehall Road, Warwick Street and Hillmorton Road.

86. Another 'snapshot' from 1896 of a family walking along Clifton Road near to the top of Bath Street, before any of the houses had been turned into shops. The Lawrence Sheriff Lower School is across the road to the right.

87. Lawrence Sheriff's intention to provide free education for the children of Rugby and Brownsover was abrogated by the Public Schools Act of 1868, and Rugby School ceased to fulfil its founder's wishes. A campaign was started by W. F. Wratislaw in 1826 and was followed up by Thomas Caldecott, who succeeded in having implemented a proposal by Dr. Temple in 1864 to set up a separate Lower School for local boys. This school, on glebe land in Clifton Road, was opened in 1878, originally taking about 60 boys. It was in a mock-Tudor style, with an effigy of a man in the livery of the London Grocers' Company, the guild to which Lawrence Sheriff belonged. This photograph was taken in 1903.

88. This house, known as Whitehall and pictured here in 1865, stood near the bottom of Whitehall Road until cleared for road widening in 1879. Originally it was probably an open-hall house with a central hearth. The walls were cob, two feet thick, carrying a braced open-framed and hipped roof with gablets to let out the smoke. These features suggest a 15th-century house of a reasonably prosperous freeman, and it was the oldest complete example at the time the photograph was taken, although divided into tenements. It may once have been an inn called the *White Horse*, for a close next to the building had that name, suggesting that 'Whitehall' may have been a corruption of 'White Horse'.

89. Clifton Road leading out of the town near the top of Winfield Street in about 1900. The lane which led up to Eastlands Farm lies to the right, now built over by Eastlands estate. The young trees lining the road were a continuation of the 1886 planting.

90.   The bridge where Clifton Road crosses Clifton (alias Moreton) Brook at the bottom of the hill has been known for generations as Butler's Leap, drawn here in about 1885. Before the road was widened in 1906, the stream looped alongside the road, on the left of the picture, before flowing under the bridge. This was the last stage of a brook-jumping run undertaken in the spring term by Rugby School boys, starting Brownsover Mill. In about 1849 a 17-year-old boy, Arthur G. Butler, cleared the fence and brook in one leap for the first time, a memorable feat not often equalled. The drawing is by George C. Richards, a native of Churchover and a pupil at the school, later become Dean of Durham.

Hillmorton Road

91. Aerial view of Hillmorton Road from the top of the tower of Rugby School Chapel, *c*.1880. The school clock tower is in the central foreground and on the left is Trinity Church overlooking the fields towards the newly-built Lawrence Sheriff School.

92.   Hillmorton Road and the Recreation Ground in 1910, before the installation of the Memorial Gates. Originally one of Stanley's fields, it was bought by the town council for a cattle market in 1874, but objections by local residents resulted in the present ground being acquired close to the L.N.W.R. station, and the field was retained as a recreation ground for the town.

93. This 28-ton armoured First World War tank was brought to Rugby by rail, driven to the Recreation Ground under its own power and installed within railings as a reminder of that conflict. It was ceremoniously named 'Cecilia' after the Countess of Denbigh in recognition of her invaluable voluntary work during the war. Later, adventurous boys used it on occasion as a climbing frame. Its engine remained in place for years, but in 1940 the tank and its railings were sold for scrap and it ended its days ignominiously under the flame-cutting torch.

The leafy country lane leading to Lower Hillmorton as was in 1910. In the Enclosure Award it was classified as a -ft.-wide bridle road, but lack of upkeep over the years uced the lower-lying stretches to a narrow muddy track, ecially where flanked by a stream. Today the lane is ered by the Abbot's Farm estate, the area shown here g between the bottom of Vere Road and Linnell Road.

Streets to the Station

95.   The view down Railway Terrace from the top of Trinity Church tower in 1880. The crowded 'Horsepool End' of Gas Street on the left of the *Grazier's Arms* can be seen. The tall chimney stack close to Railway Terrace shows the position of the early gas works, and the chimney on the left was in Over's timber yard.

96.   The Palace Theatre in Railway Terrace, 1911. Opened as a music hall seating 1,000 by Leonard Vint (posters advertising its programme can be seen in plate 63), it was renamed Vint's Hippodrome in 1913 and continued until 1922. A year later, under new management, it became the Prince of Wales Theatre, a venue for local amateur as well as professional performances until its closure in 1939.

97.   Albert Street in 1908 at the junction with Regent Street which was laid out in 1902. Opposite is the *Grand Hotel*, which opened as the *Rugby Private Hotel* in 1882, occupying the double-fronted portion with a portico seen on the left. In 1902 it was taken over, doubled in size and renamed. It remained the largest and best appointed hotel in Rugby until it was demolished in 1975 to make way for the Department of Health offices.

98.   Regent Street, *c*.1912, which was laid out in 1901 on the old Hall or Moat estate. Little has changed apart from the shop-fronts, and a pleasant variety of Edwardian architecture can be seen in the upper storeys, making this area the most homogeneous in the town. Behind the camera, the street divides and is flanked by a series of terraced houses.

99.   The cattle market at the bottom of Railway Terrace and Murray Road in 1903. It moved here in 1878 and wa[s]
extended in 1893 and 1897. In 1905 it was repaved and again enlarged in 1907 as a result of its continued prosperit[y]

Dunchurch and Barby Roads

100.   The Catholic Church on Dunchurch Road in 1864, with St Marie's College behind. It was originally a small church with a chancel, nave, north aisle and lady chapel, and a gabled tower at the south-west corner built in 1846/7 to the designs of A. W. N. Pugin. The land was donated and the whole project financed by Captain John Hibbert of Bilton Grange. He was also responsible for providing land and building a college for the Rosminian Order, again to the designs of Pugin, which opened in 1852. His son, Edward, designed the enlargement to the church carried out from 1864-7, as well as the extension of 1872.

101. Dunchurch Road leading up the hill past St
Marie's Roman Catholic Church to Rugby in 1890,
illustrating the rough gravelly surfaces of the road
and footpath with the open drainage channel
between. In 1850 the hill was lowered for easier
ascent. To the far right of the church is St Marie's
College with its seven chimney stacks, and to the
left of the road Brookside House can be seen
between the trees. At the top of the hill are the
Catholic schools and Captain Hibbert's
coach-house.

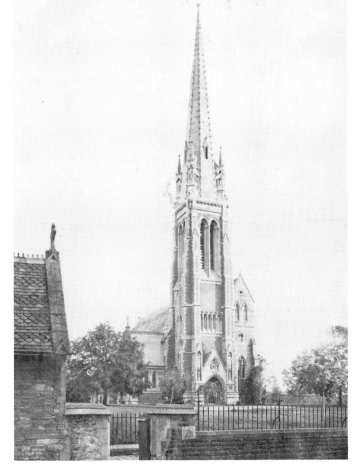

102.   One of Rugby's best-known landmarks is the
slender spire of St Marie's Church which stands
200 ft. high. Designed in the Early English style by
Bernard Whelan and built in 1872 by Parnell's, the
local builders, it included a western entrance porch
in place of one into the north aisle. The benefactor
was again Captain Hibbert who also provided an
eight-bell carillon which is still in use. This
photograph was taken in about 1910 before
gravestones were erected in the front of the
churchyard.

103. The view along Dunchurch Road in 1900. The house on the left was known as 'The Laurels' and was opened as a private school for girls in 1872 by Miss Woods. By 1936 the school had outgrown its premises and moved to Wroxall Abbey near Warwick. The Laurels was acquired by the B.T.H. Company for an apprentice hostel, but in 1963 it was bought by St Marie's Church for use as a parish club. In 1974 it was demolished in a development scheme for sheltered housing.

104. Barby Road in about 1906, with the School Close on the right. On the left, past the Temple entrance, is the ornately-turreted Temple Library House, once called the Curator's House, and home of the Art Master.

105. The water tower on Barby Road was built in 1851 on the high ground beyond the South (Sow) Brook in a scheme to provide the town with a continuous adequate water supply. The 92-ft. tower had a capacity of 56,000 gallons pumped up from an arched underground reservoir fed by drains from a gravel bed underlying the hill. It was commissioned on 31 January 1852 and built in what was considered an Italian style, faced with coloured glazed bricks. The scheme proved inadequate and, after an abortive attempt to use a deep-bore well, water was extracted from the Avon. The tower was superseded by a larger, plainer concrete structure near Ashlawn Road in 1936 and finally pulled down in 1948.

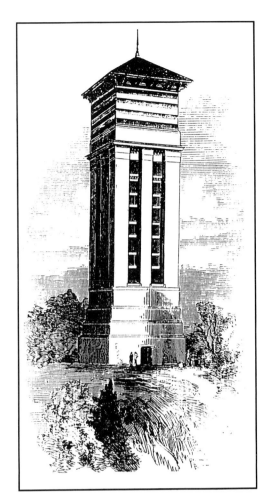

106. The old water tower on Barby Road in 1902, surrounded by its growing screen of trees. After the tower was opened in 1852, the road from there to Rugby was called Watergate Street and, having a double avenue of trees along the footpath, became a well-known 'lovers' lane'.

The Rural Scene

107.   A rural scene, drawn in 1884, looking towards Barby over Onley Fields from the bottom of Onley Lane where it fords the Rainsbrook. The footbridge was needed in times of flood. This lane is a continuation of Barby Road and formed part of the ancient Fielden Street between Rugby and Daventry. The deserted village of Onley lay to the right in the next field.

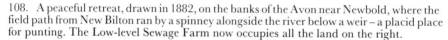

108.   A peaceful retreat, drawn in 1882, on the banks of the Avon near Newbold, where the field path from New Bilton ran by a spinney alongside the river below a weir – a placid place for punting. The Low-level Sewage Farm now occupies all the land on the right.

109. Abbot's Farm in 1938, looking towards Clifton, showing the corn stooked and gathered in by hand. The whole farm has been built over by an estate of the same name and this cornfield has been covered by Fleet, Loverock and McKinnel Crescents, illustrating the extent of urban spread since the war.

110. A peaceful stretch of the Oxford Canal near Brownsover where it is joined by the old arm above Brownsover Hall, before motor-driven narrow boats made an appearance. Here, a pair of boats is being towed by a horse led by the bargee, with no noise to disturb the quiet of the waterway.

St Andrew's Church

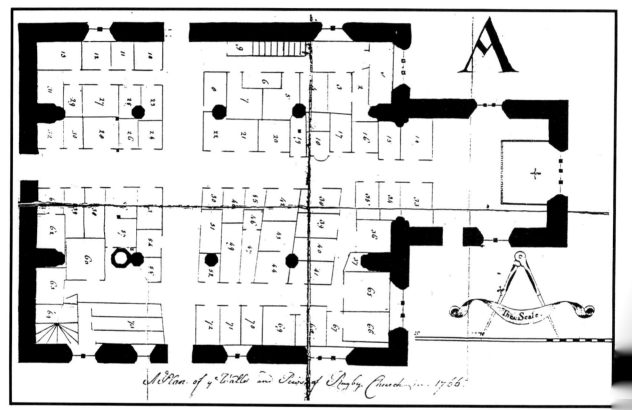

A Plan of y'e Walls and Pews of Rugby Church in 1766.

111. The succession of alterations to the parish church of St Andrew in the 18th and 19th centuries, culminating in its almost complete demolition in 1877 in preparation for rebuilding, has left little evidence of the 14th-century church and there are no surviving illustrations. This scale plan, made in 1766 for re-pewing the church, is of outstanding interest as the only record which reveals the size and structure of the medieval building, because at that date no significant changes had been made. The tower is not included and external features have been omitted, but the plan reveals a four-bay nave and aisles 54 ft. long by 45 ft. wide with a chancel 21 ft. long by 16 ft. wide. A seating schedule gives the capacity as about 400, excluding a west gallery built in 1707 for children of the Elborowe School. The old font is in front of Caldecott's pew no.60, but was discarded in the re-pewing, when the priest's door on the south side of the chancel was also blocked up. The pulpit, its stairs and the clerk's desk remained in the same place throughout all the alterations until the rebuilding.

112. This drawing by G. Mayes, once familiar to Rugbeians as the cover of the parish
magazine, shows the 14th-century tower fitting into the rebuilt church as seen from the
narrow jetty which cuts across the churchyard. This once extended a considerable way on
the left, but only a strip remains along the wall. The railed-in piece has long been paved,
and recently the footpath was widened and the area 'landscaped'.

113. This early 14th-century chest, part of the medieval church furniture, is still in the church. The back and front are tenoned into wide stiles extended to form legs but fitted with wheels for mobility. The chains may once have had long poles threaded through their rings so that the chest could be carried. It may therefore have originally been a travelling chest for the valuables of someone of rank, perhaps the lord of the manor.

114. The south side of the church in 1826. In 1814 the medieval nave and aisles were lengthened eastwards by two bays, and a new chancel was built with a vestry on the south side. This engraving of a drawing by Edward Pretty illustrates these additions as well as the geometrical tracery of the enlarged windows. The lean-to next to the vestry was the entrance to stairs leading to the gallery for the boys of Rugby School. A brick addition to the south aisle was planned in 1790 and erected in 1797.

115.   The north side of the church seen from Church Street in 1864, clearly showing the alterations of 1814. The extension to the north aisle begins where its height is raised over the two large windows in order to give adequate headroom for a gallery inside. The porch appears to be the 14th-century original.

116. The incredibly cluttered church interior *c.*1870, looking east. The south arcade was demolished in 1831 for a new south aisle, the stone piers being replaced by slim columns of cast iron by Rickmans of Birmingham, but fitted with wooden capitals! Due to the position of the pulpit, pews faced inwards and curtains screened one half from the other. The chancel and east window were almost invisible because of overhanging galleries.

117. Another interior view *c.*1870, but looking west. The first three piers of the north arcade and their arches survived from the medieval church, and still remain, albeit re-dressed in 1877. The west gallery carries a three-manual organ built by Ralph Dallam in 1664 for Queens' College, Cambridge. From there it was moved to Kings Norton Church, near Leicester, and then from a house in nearby Galby it came to Rugby in 1793, where it remained until the 1877 rebuilding.

118.   The construction of the new tower and spire in 1894, 15 years after the new church was finished. It was completed in 1895 to a height of 182 ft., less than originally planned due to foundation problems. The church and spire were designed by William Butterfield and built by the local firm Parnell and Son. Mr. George C. Benn donated the funds and provided the peal of eight bells.

119. The old Rectory House was taken over in 1954 by the William Temple College to provide courses linking Church and Industry. In 1971 the property was occupied by a marriage guidance bureau. The house appears to be of 18th-century origin, replacing an earlier timber-framed parsonage of seven bays. It has been enlarged and modified, the Beatty Survey (see plate 120) showing extensions and a wing of outbuildings. This photograph shows an addition to the south front, east of the bay window, made early this century.

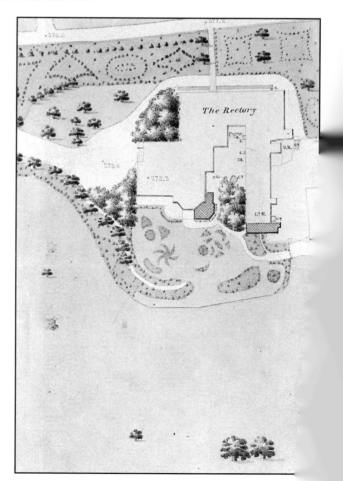

120. The rectory plan in the Beatty Survey of 1851. The east wing of outbuildings has since gone, and the south front has been extended eastwards. The hatched areas were glass conservatories.

Rugby School

121.   The south front of Rugby School from Barn Close, drawn by Edward Pretty in 1809. The apsidal building with the Venetian window was the large schoolroom known as Big School, surmounted by a hexagonal cupola. The hall and adjacent schoolroom were built by Edward Johnson, a builder on Lord Bray's estate at Stanford on Avon, in 1750 on a scale similar to the old school in Church Street.

122.   The same view in 1825 from an unfinished watercolour by Edward Rudge, who succeeded Edward Pretty as drawing master in 1824. It shows the new school built between 1809 and 1813 to the designs of Henry Hakewell. Turrets flank the projecting hall of School House, built on the site of Big School, with studies and dormitories on the right. The cupola was replaced by a battlemented square clock-tower. The rather ghost-like cricketers appear because Rudge usually filled in figures last, but abandoned this picture before that stage.

123. A little-known drawing of the school seen from School Street on the north side, showing the Burnaby manor house as it was adapted by the School before the rebuilding of 1808. It is primitive, probably the effort of a schoolboy, but is valuable in that it is likely to be true to reality. The headmaster lived in the main part of the house on the left, the open gateway leading to a courtyard and to the school hall. The gateway seems to have been close to the present Quad entrance.

124. This rare aquatint by George Hawkins shows the school in 1817 facing School Street, now Lawrence Sheriff Street. The Master's house, begun in 1809, had been recently completed, as had much of the new school further along the street beyond the Quad gateway.

125. The school seen across the Close from Barby Road in about 1880 before New Big School was built.

126. Thomas Hughes, a pupil from 1834-42 under Dr. Arnold, made Rugby and the school famous in literature through his novel *Tom Brown's Schooldays*. This commemorative white marble statue of him by Thomas Brock was unveiled in 1899 by Edward Benson, Archbishop of Canterbury, and stands in the forecourt of the Temple Library and Art Museum in Barby Road. This photograph, taken in about 1910, also shows the old locks standing at the side of the entrance.

The Railways

127. The scene at Hillmorton in June 1837, during the building of the embankment to carry the London and Birmingham Railway, looking across the canal bridge between the locks. The Oxford Canal Company's houses can be seen in the distance, the trees hiding their workshops but not the engine-house chimney. This watercolour is by Edward Rudge and was painted when he lived at Hillmorton between 1833 and 1837.

128. Another Edward Rudge view of work in progress, this time looking towards Rugby. The canal can be seen in the middle distance where the lane to Clifton rises up the hill, and it was here that the railway bridge was built.

129.   This viaduct, known locally as the Eleven Arches, was built from 1839-40 to carry the new Midland Counties Railway across the Avon valley and the Leicester road. This etching of about 1860 by Alfred Tilliman shows a train leaving Rugby over the viaduct, the turnpike to Leicester running under the second arch from the left. Beyond, on the left side of the road, can be seen the toll-house. Behind the first arch was the canal wharf, in 1840 the temporary location of the station terminus until the completion of the viaduct.

130.   The second station on the London and Birmingham Railway in Rugby was built in 1840 at the bottom of Station Terrace to accommodate the new Midland Counties line. It replaced the first station off Newbold Road but, by 1881, a third was needed to cope with the six lines which converged in Rugby. This opened 100 yards east in 1886, and the canopy seen here was re-used over its entrance. In this photograph of about 1860 the large building on the left was for the stationmaster – the man in the top hat – and the refreshment room manager.

131.   A north-bound train on platform one of the L.N.W.R. station in 1910. The sides as well as the roof were glazed for
protection against the weather, and smoke-ducts ran the length of the platform over the tracks. The placards on the
bookstall include 'Turks seize Italian Liner' and 'Navy Airship Wrecked', both confirming the date of the photogra

132. Rugby was famed for its great signal-gantry on the London side of the station, rivalled in size only by one in York.
It controlled 13 tracks and had two tiers in duplicate to ensure signal visibility against the Great Central girder bridge, se
here in the early stages of its construction. The gantry was built at Crewe by the L.N.W.R. but erected in 1896 by the Gre
Central Railway well before the bridge was built, and then maintained by them. This photograph records its completion,
with officials and the erection gang posing even on the top of the highest signal post. The heavy wooden frames behind we
aids in assembling the girder structure of the bridge. It was replaced by electric colour signalling in 1939.

133. The Great Central Railway bridge over the Oxford Canal between Brownsover and Clifton at an early stage in construction, photographed by the 'snapshot' cameraman in 1896. The sight of a boy leading a horse towing a pair of narrow boats is now a thing of the past, as is the railway here, closed in 1966.

134. The Great Central station in Hillmorton Road in 1910. It was built in 1897-8, and the line opened for coal traffic in 1898 and passenger trains in 1899. The cabs seen here assembled only when express trains were due, especially in the early days when they were infrequent.

Institutions

135. Staff leaving the offices of the B.T.H. Company in 1912. The straw-hatted men and white-bloused women are in sharp contrast to the group of three factory hands with their cloth caps.

136. The Rugby Portland Cement Works between Newbold Road and New Bilton were opened by G. H. Walker in 1865, but only became successful after being taken over by C. Hall in 1871. The photograph shows the quarry in 1890 when steam excavators were in use.

137.   The entrance to the Hospital of St Cross in 1903. The gable brickwork incorporates the initials of Richard Henry Wood J.P. and his wife Elizabeth who founded it in 1884 with a substantial endowment of £10,000. It replaced the hospital which had opened in Pennington Street in 1869 and which later moved to Castle Street.

138.   View of the hospital from the south in 1905 before a new wing, including two children's wards, was added in 1907. Since then many more additions have been made, and the field in the foreground has been turned into a car park.

139. One of the most notable additions to the hospital was this Sun Pavilion extending the length of the south front. It was opened in 1932 by Mary, the Princess Royal, and was intended for the treatment of tuberculosis patients, for whose benefit the sliding doors could be kept wide open. It has since been turned over to orthopaedic cases.

140. A carefully posed photograph of ward No.1, the men's ward, in about 1905 – still recognisable today. Notice the bed-covers carrying a large cross design.

41. There was an ad hoc body of fire-fighters in Rugby from medieval days, but in 1775 a manual fire
gine with fire-buckets was presented to the town by Henry Wilson and housed in a lean-to at
Andrew's Church. A more modern engine was obtained in 1822, kept in the old lock-up in Warwick
eet, and managed by John Bromwich, a local builder, who provided a crew from his own employees.
1875 a regular volunteer brigade was formed with an engine, fire-escape and a crew consisting of
otain, lieutenant, surgeon, turn-cock, five engineers and 18 firemen. Their horse-drawn engine is shown
e in Chapel Street in 1876, the firemen being the men without brass helmets! In 1893 a steam fire engine
s added to their equipment and in 1905 a horse-drawn fire-escape was donated.

142.   The Rugby Football Club fifteen in 1878, led by their captain W. Bradshaw (holding the ball), outside what appears to be a makeshift pavilion in their temporary ground in a field off Clifton Road. The club was formed in 1872 and played its first game in December 1872, to win against Lutterworth. Until 1877 they were called Rugby Crusaders, then Rugby Football Club, and by 1880 had moved to their permanent ground in Webb Ellis Road. At some stage in the next decade their jerseys were changed from red and black stripes to a red lion on a white ground, hence their present name – the Rugby Lions.

143.   The Rugby Cricket Club side in 1894, their Jubilee year, with the captain C. C. Mott seated at the centre. The club first met in August 1843 at Bennfield House in North Street and played their first match in 1844 on a field, now built over, between Bilton Road and Merttens Field.

144. The Rugby Town Football (soccer) Club in the 1911-12 season.

Events

145. This rather ceremonial use of the stocks is reported as being the last time they were used. 'Old' (William) Jarvis, a regular tippler, was convicted of being drunk and disorderly on a Sunday and ordered to pay five shillings with costs or to spend six hours in the stocks. He is seen here on 5 December in 1865 with a crowd of onlookers and under the watch of one of the three town constables, probably the most senior, William Haswell. The stocks and pillory were subject to heavy use and were in continual need of repair, replacement of locks and fresh coats of paint.

146. The pioneer aviator, Claude Grahame-White (1879-1959), landing his Henry Farman III biplane in a field at Normandy Farm, Hillmorton, in the early morning of 23 April 1910. It was his first stop in an attempt to fly from London to Manchester within 24 hours in response to a *Daily Mail* offer of £20,000 for the first aviator to succeed. However, gales stopped his journey in Lichfield and his only rival, Louis Paulham, made the flight four days later to take the prize money, although the French Aero Club awarded Grahame-White their gold medal.

147.   A profusion of flags in High Street to welcome Edward VII on his visit to open the new Temple Speech Room on 3 July 1909. The king often visited Rugby as the guest of Mrs. Arthur James at her Coton House home near Churchover.

148.   Regent Street decorated for the visit of Edward VII in 1909, at a time when almost every household and shop kept a store of flags for such events.

149.   A great crowd filling Church Street for the memorial service for Edward VII in 1910. This photograph provides interesting study in the dress of the time.

MEMORIAL SERVICE
H.M. KING EDWARD VII

150. The Armistice parade on Saturday 16 November 1918, leaving the Recreation Ground and turning into
Whitehall Road. The procession was led by the police force and the band of Rugby School O.T.C.; the section seen
is led by Capt. C. H. Fuller and Rugby Town Volunteers. The Town and Works fire brigades are in line along
Hillmorton Road, waiting their turn to enter the parade.

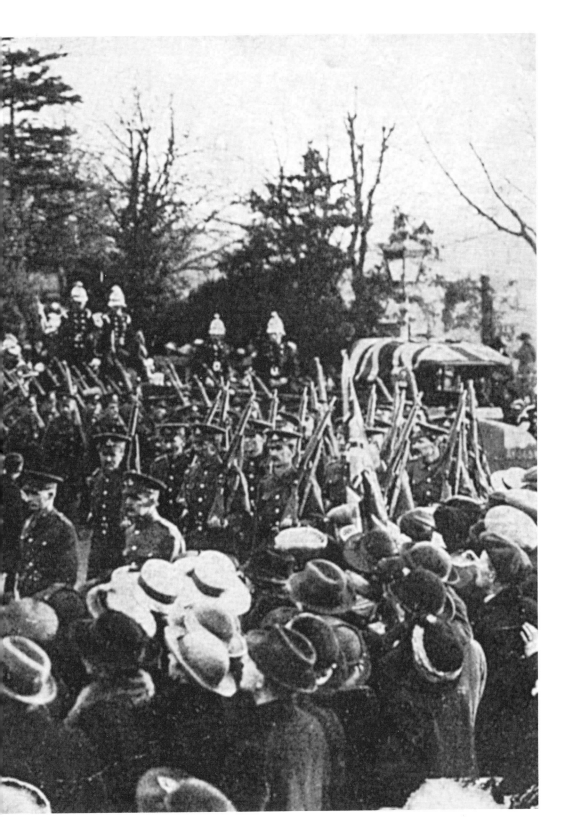

151. Celebrating the Armistice on 16 November 1918, finishing with a march-past in the Recreation Ground at Hillmorton Road. Lt. Col. F. F. Johnstone is taking the salute from the Rugby Town Volunteer Corps led by Capt. C. H. Fuller. This was the final stage in a long parade through the town.

152. Celebrating the Armistice in an open-air service at the clock tower, led by massed brass bands conducted by E. R. Stebbing. The occasion is notable for the total absence of bunting and flags.

. The unveiling of the War Memorial Gates at the entrance to the Hillmorton Road Recreation Ground by Field-
rshal Earl French of Ypres on Sunday 12 March 1922. The gates were dedicated by Dr. A. A. David, Bishop of
Edmundsbury and Ipswich, former headmaster of Rugby School. They were moved further east to make way for a road
through the grounds to a sports centre.

154. Crowds converging on Market Place for the open-air thanksgiving for Queen Victoria's Diamond Jubilee on 22 June 1897.

155. Queen Victoria's Diamond Jubilee, 1897.

156. The visit of King Edward VII, 1909.

157. The Silver Jubilee of King George V in 1935, with a flower display around the base of the Clock Tower and seating for the brass band.

158. A strikingly modern design at the Clock Tower for the coronation of Queen Elizabeth II in 1953. It was the work of A. C. Kemp, head of the art department at Rugby College of Technology and Arts, using 872 electric light bulbs illuminate the crown surmounting the tower and with floodlighting installed at the base.